DELUSIONAL, FOR GOD'S SAKE!

by

Judy K. Feder, "M.D."

Factor Press
Post Office Box 8888
Mobile, Alabama 36689

ISBN 1-887650-13-X

Publisher's Cataloging-in-Publication

Feder, Judy
     Delusional, for Gods's Sake!
       p. cm.
     ISBN 1-887650-13-X

         1. Manic-depressive illness. 2. Psychoses. 3.
         Delusion. 4. Depression, Mental.
1.   Title
RC 516.F44 D45 1998

TABLE OF CONTENTS

ACKNOWLEDGMENTS

My story would never have reached print had it not been for Allen, my husband, who read, edited and reread and reedited it so many times that he has it committed to memory. Marion Lowing, editor, writer and critic, directed Allen's efforts onto the right tracks. Bob Henry, journalist, writer, and gentleman extraordinary, polished those tracks until they gleamed. Of course, had it not been for Gilbert R. Ladd, IV, M.D., my story would have concluded chapters earlier with my obituary.

PREFACE

I had you goin' for a minute there, didn't I, when you saw the M.D. after my name as the author of this book? In this case, the M.D. stands for manic-depressive. Now you are probably wondering what does a manic-depressive want to write about, or who cares, or can manic-depressives even write? If so, what could they say that could possibly be worth taking up your reading time? Well, you will have to read this book to find out. It's all true, although I should define my view of "depressive." I am a certified manic, but have never become depressed following a manic binge as the psychiatrists say I should. (However, many of the drugs psychiatrists have given me produced depressive side effects.)

This book is an autobiography interwoven with bits about others I have met along the way, persons ranging from those I believe have triggered some of my manic attacks to those who "cured" me. You'll also find sketches of the hospital inmates, hospital staffs and others. I have used pseudonyms throughout to protect those who have had to deal with me in times of crisis.

You'll discover hope and despair, humor and sorrow, failure and success, fact and philosophy, and a growth of faith unhindered by the mechanics, rituals and fanatic fundamentalism invented by man.

I have been to the mountain top and I have been in hell. Believe me, the mountain top is better. All of my life I had been told that you "can't beat the system." Well, I found that with the help of God you not only can beat the system, you can change it for the better.

By training and experience I am a teacher, a career choice I made when very young. The desire to teach is strong within me, as is the belief that you learn better through kindness, humor and understanding than you do with the paddle. If by reading this you learn of and empathize with a side of life other than what comes out of your TV, movie screens or magazines, then I will have succeeded as a teacher. If what you learn spurs you to action, I will have succeeded as a very effective teacher, and perhaps even a tool of God. This does not mean I'm a religious fanatic, or a stalwart of some advocacy group.

It means it is the work of someone who agrees with George Bernard Shaw when he wrote, "You see things and you say, 'Why?' But I dream things that never were and I say, 'Why not?'"

During my battles, I have been hospitalized or committed to hospitals many times. Some of those have mercifully disappeared from my memory. I will recount here only those that remain vivid or became part of a learning experience, showing me another side of life. I now understand what dirt, hunger, thirst, loneliness, boredom, poverty and degradation are. Lockups (solitary confinement) strengthened me and my faith. I was never really alone. God was always with me. He even permitted me to believe that there were movie cameras outside the little windows found in every cell door. They were focused on me. I heard God's voice, "Pretend that this room is not a cell. Ignore the cracked walls, chipped paint, the smell of urine, the lack of freedom. This is a movie set and you're the star. Make me proud of you. Show in this film what you've learned about life, fighting unhappiness with strength and vigor, enduring and overcoming obstacles and not losing your sense of humor. This is the message I want on film."

Now it was all clear to me. Now I understood. We were making a movie of my life and I was playing me. I would give a great performance, and my audience, my critic, was God. It was a thrilling experience. I had always been "on stage" when teaching and loved theater and movies. Now I had a chance to express myself. And believe me, I did. My manic mind was very creative and I assumed the role as directed. I couldn't let them sedate me. I had to be awake to perform. I now readily see that I was delusional, but it was "Delusional, for God's Sake."

Judy Feder

Chapter 1

I SHOULD BE DEAD

In August of 1995, my husband Allen and I moved from Huntsville to Mobile, Alabama. Always the logical one, he programmed the shift from north to south Alabama on his computer. It worked, and within a month my dad visited with us and we had a wonderful month with him, learning about our new home town together. His return to Philadelphia left a void. This, coupled with the fact that, unknowingly, my lithium medication was no longer being properly assimilated in my system, led to my entering upon a severe manic spiral. In one weekend, I fought with Allen (when he interfered with my contacting the local media to announce my selection by God as the new messiah), drove him out of our apartment with my obnoxious behavior, bought a new car, gave large sums of money to strangers in sleazy restaurants, and to this day don't know what other foolish acts I committed. Allen would tell me about some of them later, but here was the big one:

I was hearing voices, saying things like, "Judy, you have a mission and it must be accomplished soon." I believed that God had chosen me, for some unknown reason, to save the U.S. from further decay. I methodically planned my presidential campaign, had refreshed my Spanish so I could appeal to Latino voters, scribbled endless notes concerning my platform for the New World Party—"All the Way with J.A.K." (My maiden name was Judy Arlene Kaniss.)

I would "outlaw all the negative newspaper headlines, TV talk shows like Capital Gang, and emphasize, publicize and reward all that is good in America."

"Why not," I scribbled, "utilize a great source of intelligent manpower—senior citizens? Encourage and reward our seniors and their participation as volunteers in our public schools (VIPS)."

I attacked the matter of physical fitness. "Revamp, revitalize and renew the exercises that will fight disease and obesity. Get rid of the flabby American!" And while you're at it, "Put a heavy tax on junk food, and subsidize healthy foods."

And I struck a blow for conservation. "There should be less waste—save our forests, beaches, cities, slums; preserve what is good, get rid of what is bad, think before you toss."

I also suggested that somehow we clean up politics so every child would "want and dream of being president."

But my immediate problem was to find a way to gain recognition of my own presidential candidacy. As if on cue, another voice told me to "start driving and stop where I tell you to. Have no fear. I will be with you. Follow my instructions and you will have a forum for my message."

I got into my new car and, with my minimal sense of direction, started driving. The next thing I remember seeing was a sign marking the Pascagoula, Mississippi, exit. I was heading west on the heavily traveled Interstate 10, but wasn't aware of it. I only *felt* that it was here I should lie down on the highway to stop traffic. When there were enough people, I could stir them up in time to make the next radio and TV newscasts!

During those broadcasts I would announce my candidacy for President of the United States. After all, I was a citizen, certainly over 35 years of age, a history and political science teacher and the possessor of common sense and analytical skills. Didn't that make me the logical choice of voters for getting the job done?

I wasn't aware of where I was, and didn't bother to wait for another voice. I pulled my car off the road, got out and walked to the center lane of westbound traffic. There I lay down and stretched out to interrupt as much traffic flow as possible. The cacophony of horns and screeching brakes was muted in my brain. The motorists swerving around me created a kaleidoscope of lights and colors.

Then came the blast of a trucker's air horn and the earthquake-like way his braking tires grabbed at the paving and wrinkled the asphalt. That was when I recognized that I was in some danger, but still felt no fear. God was right there with me, wasn't He?

I found confirmation in the scream of sirens and the flashing blues of the State Highway Patrol cruisers. My police escort had arrived! I opened my eyes in short-lived triumph. No reporters. No cameras. No microphones. Just a pair of burly state troopers glaring at me from under their wide-brimmed hats.

"Are you hurt, lady?" one asked.

"No," I declared with proper dignity. "I'm waiting for the crowd and the reporters before I make my announcement as a presidential candidate."

"Not on my highway, you don't!" The officers glanced at each other with raised eyebrows, then hoisted me to my feet and marched me off the asphalt. "That your car?" the one who had claimed highway ownership asked.

"Yes!" I screamed as I struggled to break free.

"Give me the keys!"

I shook my head and started kicking with all my might.

"Give me the damned keys!"

"They're in the car," a third trooper shouted.

"We've got a wild one on our hands," the officer in

charge declared. "Radio ahead—" He relaxed his hold just enough for me to get off a wild, swift kick to his groin. I vaguely remember that his next order was accompanied by a string of profanity, but it's content failed to sink in.

I know they handcuffed me and shoved me unceremoniously into the caged backs eat of the patrol car.

"God sent me!" I screamed as I pounded on the wire cage and kicked at the unforgiving doors. "He calls me his messiah to save the world!"

I was made a guest of the state of Mississippi in what seemed to be a pest hole of a jail cell—graffiti on the walls, a broken sink, a leaking commode, a torn and filthy mattress on a rusted metal bunk.

The shock of all this gave me partial sanity. "How did I get here?" I asked myself aloud. "By now I'm supposed to be on TV. What is a middle-aged, middle-class, fairly bright Jewish girl doing in orange prison clothes and sitting in a filthy Mississippi jail cell?"

I screamed, "Let me out of here!" No one answered. Then I thought, "Maybe if I sing they'll listen to me." But when I sang at the top of my lungs, no one responded. Mercifully, my mind has blanked out the rest of that episode. I later found that I had been charged with everything from disorderly conduct and interfering with traffic to assaulting an officer of the law.

I was kept in jail overnight, until someone realized that they had a person with a mental problem on their hands. Then they took me to the psychiatric ward of the local hospital where I was placed in seclusion. Since I have always reacted violently to seclusion, I *remained* in seclusion.

When Allen realized that I hadn't returned home the night I had left, he contacted the Mobile Police Department, the Sheriff's office, then the Alabama Highway Patrol. All points bulletins were issued. Just when Allen began losing his usual composure, he received a phone call from the Pascagoula police telling him where I was and what had happened. This began an ordeal for him, daily 140 mile round trips between Mobile and Pascagoula to visit me in the hospital. He made additional trips to confer with the court-appointed psychiatrists and with lawyers who were representing me for the various charges that had been brought against me.

At the same time he was trying to arrange for me to be transferred to a Mobile facility, but there were no beds available in Mobile.

On the tenth morning of my stay in Mississippi, Allen made his usual call from our home for the required permission to visit with me that day. He was told that he'd better get to the hospital soon since I was being permanently transferred that day to the Mississippi State Mental Institution in Meridian. The reason—I was "beyond hospital control."

Stunned, he hung up the phone, only to have it ring again. A bed had opened up in a hospital in Mobile, but it had to be claimed before noon of that day or the court would "award" it to someone else. It was then 9:00 a.m. Allen began a frantic rush to get the Mississippi court to release me to the Mobile hospital on condition that I undergo more treatment.

Of course he had to drive the 70 miles to hospital to pick me up before the van arrived to take me to Meridian. Then he had to bring me back to Mobile before the hospital bed was lost.

He accomplished it all with dozens of long distance phone calls and some race car driving through heavy traffic and occasional 50-mile-an-hour crosswinds.

Later, when I asked him how he did it, he said, "God was my co-pilot." I remember nothing of Allen's transporting me from Pascagoula to Mobile. Before the hospital staff in Mississippi would let Allen move me, they sedated me heavily and wrapped me in restraints so that I couldn't jump out of the car or wrest its control from Allen.

I was in the Mobile hospital for six weeks. In spite of the Mississippi authorities wanting my stay to be mandatory, Alabama law made it voluntary, which meant I could leave any time I chose to do so.

I wanted out, and Allen had great difficulty convincing

me to stay until I regained some normalcy. My psychiatrist at the time had been treating me with Tegritol, saying he found lithium to be less effective for me.

He finally consented to my release, but with the admonition that I was to visit him for needed treatments on a scheduled basis. I ignored his wishes and less than three months later had to be confined to another Mobile mental hospital. This was traumatic, but also blessed me with the care of Dr. Gilbert R. Ladd IV, whom I learned to believe was God-sent.

This entire odyssey could have had a much earlier and abrupt ending. But for God, my lying down on the pavement of heavily traveled Interstate 10 would have resulted in instant death. I contrast the entire traumatic episode with my present, quiet and peaceful life. With the care of God, and those through whom He works—Allen with his love, patience and wisdom; Dr. Ladd with his empathy, skill and brilliance; and my father, who is just always there for me—I no longer need delusional aspirations to be a messiah or the president. I am already at the pinnacle, under God, with my trinity of Allen, Dr. Ladd and my father.

Chapter 2

I'M A MANIC BUT I LEAD
A NORMAL LIFE

A manic person has an amazing amount of physical and creative energy. It may manifest itself in many ways. Manic persons have become famous musicians, comedians, artists, writers. When they are famous enough, they are usually referred to as gifted, eccentric, precocious—anything but manic.

Those experiencing mania often see things differently than they do at other times. Sometimes the vision and mind of the manic individual becomes distorted by other manic symptoms such as inability to sleep, loss of appetite, lack of patience, irritability, and argumentativeness. The manic person may rush from activity to activity, never stopping to relax and think things over. Persons experiencing mania can literally wear themselves out and destroy their creative inspiration and thought.

I believe that manic people may be able to channel their creativity and maintain control. If they can come to understand their symptoms and behavior patterns, they and their loved ones can act on this knowledge and keep their creative behavior functioning without accelerating into social adversity. They can avoid the destruction and hospitalization that might become inevitable under uncontrolled conditions. Later chapters provide more details about attaining and maintaining a normal life, if there is such a thing, but for now...

A first step in maintaining control is a good diet. This is, of course, important at all times for everyone, but especially for a manic. Nourishing, healthy food which is low in sugar should be temptingly presented.

The manic person must not go without sleep. Using prescribed sleeping medications, that do not have too many side effects, to promote regular sleeping habits could prove a godsend for persons having manic tendencies.

Lithium and lithium alternatives such as Depakote and Tegretol help keep things on an even keel for most persons suffering bipolar disorder (manic depression), although you will later read why none of these worked for me.

Blood level tests of lithium, or its equivalents should be requested by the mania sufferer at the first signs of a "high." This is somewhat difficult because that person is probably enjoying his or her high and doesn't particularly want it regulated or curbed.

The manic person should be encouraged to take time out from all of his or her projects to relax. Exercise, in moderation, such as taking periodic long walks, is excellent for interrupting manic behavioral spiraling.

Manic persons should try to decrease their verbalizing. They usually think they're authorities on everything. A conversation soon becomes a monologue, with the manic doing all the talking. This can quickly get on people's nerves.

Manic people need to keep their possessions as well as their thoughts in order. Chaos and confusion usually bring out the bad aspects of mania.

They should learn to communicate their feelings and ideas to someone close. It doesn't necessarily have to be a professional. This encourages empathetic and sympathetic bonding.

Those who are manic need, above all, a lot of love. Showing love to a manic can at times appear impossible because the manic person comes on so strong and is so opinionated and sometimes downright obnoxious that the behavior can destroy feelings of love and caring. Giving the manic person lots of love is, nevertheless, essential toward altering his or her behavior. Giving love in the beginning of an episode is far less arduous than the effort required in communicating with the person once the condition has progressed.

Mildly manic persons have a lot to offer to the world. Their mania has led to great breakthroughs in science, engineering, and politics. But this condition must be understood thoroughly, and behavior must be regulated and channeled for the benefits to be derived. Under those circumstances, manic may be a God-given touch of genius rather than an abhorrent touch of hell. Which it will be usually rests with the manic's family, friends and associates rather than with someone experiencing mania.

Chapter 3

I'M IN GOOD COMPANY

What do Winston Churchill, Wolfgang Amadeus Mozart, Ernest Hemingway, Abraham Lincoln, Martin Luther, Michaelangelo, Patty Duke, Vivien Leigh, and Judy K. Feder have in common?

The answer is that they all were said by their more recent biographers to be afflicted with manic depressive psychosis, currently called bipolar disorder or syndrome. It is estimated that at least three percent and possibly as high as eight to ten percent of the American population suffers from manic-depression.

The best way to understand the illness is to consider its different stages of development. At the beginning of the manic state the earliest symptoms are generally quite pleasant for the victims, including increased confidence and capability. The victims are usually extremely happy, become more active and experience accelerated thought processes, which they are quick to verbalize with gusto. Their perception and creative abilities are enhanced.

When I am in that first stage of mania, it's great! I feel as though I'm on an elevator going straight up. I become talkative and verbally uninhibited. My creative abilities soar. I want to write a book, compose poetry, be a college professor of history, be an actress, scale great heights. Sometimes I will go on shopping sprees. I will make lengthy long distance telephone calls without regard for cost. Invariably, those calls aggravate those who are close to me as well as mere acquaintances. In the first stage of mania, I lean toward delusional grandeur; I am God-chosen to save the world; I will be the first Jewish woman to become president of the United States.

When the mania goes unchecked into more advanced stages I can go many days without sleep. I talk continually and am always on the go. In this stage I start getting on people's nerves, and they may react drastically. In summary, the early forms of mania are exhilarating for me, but can quickly become a strain on those around me.

When I'm in the advanced stages I act impulsively and make bad decisions. My energy is not productive.

It is poorly directed into the wrong channels. I may park across three lanes of rush hour traffic on a busy street so that, in my delusional role as God's appointed helper, I will prevent "bad" people from going to work. I leap from one frantic act to another. I'm almost incoherent in expressing my ideas. Yet I will have developed a fantastic recall and distorted reasoning ability that stimulates me to argue with the skill of a Philadelphia lawyer with anyone trying to verbally restore me to normalcy.

Invariably, by the time I reach acute mania I will be in some hospital, singing and dancing and yelling until the given sedatives take their various effects. Eventually I will enter a chemically induced sleep, then wake up incoherent and irritable, with the pattern continuing until I'm cured.

After struggling with bipolar syndrome for the past twenty-five years, I've learned to live with its attacks, and, between them, to lead a normal life. My greatest battle was coming to a thorough understanding of the condition and its symptoms. For this I will always be indebted to a psychiatrist in

Houston, Texas. In 1982 she first treated my condition as being a product of a chemical deficiency in my blood and started me on lithium medication. That enabled me to live a normal life for almost ten years.

My experiences have been such, however, that I recognize many other people become slightly manic at times. The irony in this is that for some, a mild bout with mania can earn them such appellations as "creative," "innovative," and "genius."

In this, my story, I tell you of my progressions from normalcy (if there is such a condition) to the world of mania (with its drive and creativity) to a world of sickness of the mind and body and finally a return to accepted behavior. This type of progression, I believe, has been recounted several times by others. It is the way-stations along the route I followed, however, that I believe will interest you. And the fact that I survived so much along the way to overcome many obstacles and even life-threatening occurrences.

Chapter 4

RAH! RAH! RAH! RAMONE

June, 1962

Attending Camp Ramone at the age of fifteen was when my childhood ended. The camp was in the mountains of eastern New York state, and was my first taste of a mental health facility. My parents were very proud of my earning half a scholarship (around $300.00) from my synagogue. My mother nagged me until I finally agreed to go, in spite of my trepidations. And my father bought me new clothes (I wore a size eight when I boarded the bus).

The boredom, bad food, stupidity and regimentation made it an extremely difficult experience for me.

It was and still may be a Jewish summer camp, not really a mental hospital. It was a religious camp, but in later years I would liken it to a mental hospital.

The girls (I thought of them as inmates) were snobby and cruel.

"Gee, Judy, don't you know that those shoes went out of style with the cavemen?"

They'd all been there in previous summers and had staked out the territory and all the boys.

"Hi, Will. Hi, Don. I don't know anything about canoeing. If either of you are free this afternoon, could you give me a lesson?"

"Sorry, Judy. Don't you know we've been teaming up with Selma and Joan for the last three years? Keep asking around and maybe you'll find someone who isn't committed."

I buried myself in a copy of *Gone With the Wind*, which was battered and torn by the end of the season. Rhett Butler made the boredom, classes and cliques bearable.

The boredom was the worst, and it sent me to the canteen with the money my parents had given me. I began to munch candy bars on a steady basis, substituting them for affection and friendship. My clothes began to get tight—I thought they were shrinking in the wash. Poor, gullible me. My bunk mates made sure to tell me that I cried in my sleep.

"What's the matter, Judy? Your crying and moaning kept us awake half the night. Hasn't the little girl learned to grow up?"

I didn't believe such barbs until I looked in the mirror to find my eyelids red and swollen, my cheeks streaked. This started me on a new daily ritual, waking up before my roommates did and dousing my face with cold water. By the end of the summer, I needed size 16 clothes, hated swimming lessons, and was very confused.

This place not only turned me against camp, but against organized religion.

Chapter 5

PRELUDE

My birthplace was Philadelphia, well deserving of all W. C. Fields' jokes. I was born in 1946 and raised in a small, red brick row-house having three small bedrooms and one smaller bathroom. Sam, my father, is in his 90's. He still lives there, and peddles his antique bicycle around the neighborhood every day. I was the eldest of three sisters and a brother. With my parents, this was quite a crowd for a house of this size.

I was the ugly duckling. At least that is the way I perceived myself. Helene, my second oldest sister was (and still is) slim, trim, and pretty, and she had all the boyfriends. I was constantly reminded of my plainness by living in her shadow. The phone always rang for her. I'd receive calls only from schoolmates concerned with homework and forthcoming exams. I couldn't understand why boys never noticed me at school. I now believe it was because I had no self-confidence. I was very shy and afraid to talk to boys. I buried myself in my school work, became an all A student and finally the DAR National High School History Award winner. But I would have traded all of the honors for a date to the Senior Prom. It was the most important event of a girl's high school existence.

If a person were not to be a complete and absolute social failure, he or she needed a live, breathing prom date. It didn't matter if the date was provided by a relative, was too short or was flown in by parents looking for their child's happiness. Without a date for this mega event you might as well buy a one way ticket to Siberia and take all your worldly possessions with you.

My mother constantly reassured me that the prom meant nothing. "You won't even remember it years from now," she said.

But for three months before the prom I had to constantly listen to my female classmates chatter about their dresses and dates. I don't know how I made it through those months. It seemed so important that I prayed to God every day that the phone would ring with an invitation, but to no avail. The day of the prom arrived. It was November 22, 1963. Nothing had turned up.

Three of my equally unlucky girlfriends and I decided to go to a movie to drown our sorrows that Friday night. All of the banners at the school read, "Remember November 22." They referred to the prom. But I still remember—for a different reason.

John F. Kennedy was assassinated that morning. And it changed my point of view. It showed me how relatively unimportant and insignificant my prom troubles were in comparison to losing a President in so violent a fashion. The assassin's bullet made John F. Kennedy a martyr in my eyes. My tragedy of not being invited to the prom had been lost in the nation's tragedy. The event taught me to put things in perspective and to try to keep them there. I was really stunned by it. History, which had always been my favorite subject, was being played out on TV. I had blown things out of proportion concerning the prom, a mistake which I didn't repeat for a long, long time.

l graduated from high school the following spring. And I thought graduation would mean getting away from catty girls and the frustrations of missing social occasions.

I, like many other of my school's graduates, decided to go to Temple University, located right in the heart of Philadelphia's ghetto. It was a city school. I had to travel on two buses and a sub-way to get there.

Five months at Temple University firmly convinced me I'd never have any confidence or happiness if I didn't get away from the same people I'd felt inferior to in high school.

That summer I looked through college catalogs for a change. My criteria were simple. The school had to have more boys than girls (smart, eh?), require relatively low tuition, and possess a nice campus atmosphere.

I applied to UCLA, Penn State and Michigan State University. Actually, I misread the catalog, thought I was applying to the University of Michigan instead of Michigan State University. I'm sure the officials at MSU were confused when they received an envelope containing nothing but a check, but they cheerfully sent an application urging me to apply. I returned to the catalog, discovered that my boy-girl ratio and low tuition criteria could be satisfied, and that the MSU campus was like a park.

Two weeks later, my father and I were on a plane headed for the midwest.

The summer of 1965 was important for me. I decided that if I was going to start a new life at MSU, I needed a new person-ality and a new slim figure to go with it. I went to a diet doctor who gave me some advice (which I promptly forgot), and an envelope full of pills (which I took). And miraculously, they cut my weight from a pudgy 160 pounds to a more desirable 120 pounds. That was the thinnest I'd ever been. I thought it was too good to be true; a new figure for a new beginning. My uncle even bought me a whole new size ten wardrobe.

I looked great. I felt great. When the plane landed in East Lansing, I was truly the new Judy with no more terrible feelings of inferiority. I liked MSU and myself and became optimistic about life in general. I could be anybody or anything I wanted. I could create my own future.

My father, who was then and continued to be my greatest supporter, looked around the campus and found ten different maps of MSU. He stapled them to the bulletin board in my dorm room, failing to take into account that map reading was never my forte.

MSU at that time had very few Jewish students. My father tactfully suggested we go to the campus Hillel House (a gathering place for Jewish students) and check it out. That sounded good to me—and it was! Three boys took my phone number. One of them was a thin, quiet young man named Barry Kolter. He phoned me and we started dating. He treated me very nicely. This and his manners built up my ego. We dated for football games, concerts and plays. In spring, we lay on the grass and listened to music. We talked on the phone for hours. I loved him for loving me. He caused a permanent change in me.

The only cloud that year was that much of the weight I had lost returned, and all the new clothes my uncle had bought me were too tight.

But I had Barry, and that made everything all right. The year ended, and since he was also from Philadelphia, we returned together. And Barry gave me an engagement ring.

I believed I was too young to get married, knew this was precipitous. He took me to visit his family. His mother started interfering from the moment we met, and this added to my doubts.

His mother created a scene concerning where his loyalties should be. I threw the engagement ring right at him. I may have believed I was inferior, but not so much so that I needed to be tied to a momma's boy. Exit Barry Kolter, which left a great void in my life.

I was lonely again. Somehow, I got through the summer and went back to MSU to pick up the pieces. I needed someone to replace Barry, someone to tell me I was great. My experiences before Barry left me a sucker for praise.

I thought I would find a replacement for Barry working in the graduate dorm cafeteria. What better place to meet older male students? That's where I met Stuart Stoddard. He was a heckler who showed up more and more frequently.

"This salad doesn't have enough tomatoes," he'd complain. Or, "Can't you give me a little more cake?" He was downright annoying, but at least he noticed me. That was good enough. Still, I should have recognized him for what he was. I mistook his cockiness as self-assurance, rather than what it actually was—a little person trying to be bigger than he was.

We started dating, and he became a replacement for my lost love.

I don't remember much of our courtship. It may be that my memory is selectively and blessedly merciful. We were together until the beginning of summer, when Stuart went to Phoenix and I returned to Philadelphia.

At the end of summer, my parents and I flew to Phoenix (a girl had to have a chaperone back then) and we all drove back to Philadelphia together. Stuart proposed to me in Tucumcari, New Mexico, and we were married on March 26, 1967, the start of a turbulent relationship.

In June we moved to Houston, Texas, where Humble Oil, Stuart's new employer, was located. I found a teaching position in suburban Houston's Armour Independent School District and threw myself into my work. I found that my fifth graders were a lot more appreciative of my qualities than was my husband. He wasn't very supportive of my teaching career and, regardless of my needs, worked at his job all hours.

I concentrated on being the best possible teacher. I certainly wasn't missing anything at home. My performance in class and my training in history was enough to convince District supervisors to promote me to teaching senior high history and government.

My career dreams had come true. I worked in Armour for one year, but then decided I wanted a child. I took a year off and Jamie was born in April of 1972.

I enjoyed taking care of her. She was such a good baby. But I missed the classroom in the same way an actress misses the stage. Ideas that I wanted to try out were going through my mind. When Jamie was just five months old I went back to teaching.

Maybe it was too soon, but I needed the captive audiences of my classroom.

Chapter 6

ON CENSORSHIP IN TEACHING, A SUPPORTIVE HUSBAND, AND BEING APPROPRIATE

In 1973 I was 27 years old, the mother of a beautiful six-month-old daughter, happily married (or so others thought), and, proudly, a high school history teacher.

Looking back, I can see that there were some warning symptoms heralding the first onslaught of mania. I was overly creative, needed little sleep, lost weight, and talked continuously.

In April, my life began to unravel. The school district I worked for was, in my opinion, provincial in attitudes. The principal was a former athletic coach whose attitude suggested that he intensely disliked and mistrusted students. He singled me out to complain about my approach to teaching history. This shocked me—I considered that I had developed effective and creative study plans. I based this on my students' actions and reactions.

The principal continued his criticism, and one day gave me a real jolt when he said, "I've gotten complaints from three parents about that book you assigned, *The Fixer.* They said it's about a pimp fixing up girls." He slammed his hand to the desk. "You're going to have to tell your students to close the book."

Previously, I had assigned *Nicholas and Alexandra* for extra reading while teaching about Czarist and Communist Russia. But I decided that that book painted too favorable a picture of the Czar, and switched to Bernard Malamud's *The Fixer*. I believed this would illustrate the darker side of the Czar's reign. *The Fixer* is the story of a Jewish handyman who is accused of killing a Christian girl and using her blood in a religious ritual. The man is imprisoned and kept in horrible conditions while he struggles to maintain his dignity.

"You're being unreasonable," I challenged the coach-turned-principal. "*The Fixer* is an excellent book, and it's not about prostitutes." In exasperation I added, "Tell me who the parents are, and I'll explain it to them."

"No," he snapped. "You're going to have to tell your students to stop reading it."

"I can't do that! I just completed a unit about book burning in Nazi Germany. Now, how can I tell my students to shut a book?"

"If you don't, you won't have a job."

"In that case, I resign!"

I stayed at home the next day and wrote a letter to my students. I wanted to explain the conflict that had arisen and why I was fighting for my cause. My classes had already been taken over by the department head, a close associate of the principal.

I finished the letter and arrived at the school in time for my last class. Because so many rumors had been circulating, the students were delighted to see me. The letter I began distributing read in part:

Dear Students:

You know how much I love my students, and teaching, but I cannot work under a person who runs this school like a totalitarian regime. He has insufficient respect for teachers or students. This man had pictures cut out of *Time* magazine, pictures that showed scenes from a movie, *The Grapes of Wrath.* He has ordered me to tell you to stop reading *The Fixer.* We must take a stand against these practices...

As I handed the letter to the students, the principal burst in and demanded, "Mrs. Stoddard, I'm ordering you to stop!" Then, concentrating on the students, he went on, "Can't you see what she's doing? She's exploiting you. Go with your new teacher to her room!"

The students remained at their desks in silent defiance.

"Boys and girls, do you want to wreck your school careers? Do you want to be expelled from athletics and the band?"

A few students began to leave the room. Others hesitated, then also left.

Finally, the last one started for the door. Turning first to the principal, she said, "I hate you." Then turning toward me with tears in her eyes, she said, "Mrs. Stoddard, I'm sorry I let you down."

I wanted to hug her, but merely said, "You didn't let me down. I'm proud that you lasted as long as you did."

When she was gone, the principal let loose with a tirade verging on violence. I told him I would fight him over the issue and he dared me to try.

That night when I related the events to Stuart, he sided with the principal. "You were wrong," he said bluntly. "This is what you deserve for mouthing off. When are you going to learn to control your temper?"

The next day was Saturday, and I met with some of the parents of my outraged students. They were also appalled by the principal's tactics, and promised to have a lawyer look into restoring my job.

But I did have a break. My father had been in Texas on a business trip, and stopped by our home in Houston while on his way back to Philadelphia. I begged him to take me to an

Israeli exposition at a Houston synagogue. I wanted to get the entire school experience off my mind. My father objected, saying he thought I should rest instead. He believed that I had been under too great a strain. However, I prevailed and he and I went to the exposition.

Once there, I insisted on having my picture taken with the police officer at the door. Once again, my father objected. Somehow ill at ease.

As we looked at the exhibits, I saw a breathtaking white Israeli wedding dress. I turned to my father and asked, "Daddy, will you buy me this wedding dress?"

"But Judy, it costs over three hundred dollars!"

"Please, Daddy, please! I'll pay you back! Oh, and I'll need a Star of David and an Israeli flag to go with it! Please, Daddy!" Perhaps not knowing how else to respond to his distraught daughter, my father again relented.

At home I rushed into the bedroom to try on the prized gown. I combed my hair and put on cosmetics befitting a young Israeli bride. While I did so, Stuart, my father, and two friends conferred in another part of the house. Stuart called a psychiatrist and asked for advice. The psychiatrist prescribed a sedative and advised that I be taken to a nearby hospital.

Soon afterward I came prancing into the living room wearing the wedding gown and Star of David and waving the Israeli flag. My friend, Lurine, approached me.

"Honey, you've got to get some sleep. I want you to drink this."

"I don't need anything," I protested. "I'm already tired."

"Come into the bedroom and drink this, Judy."

"Okay, if it will make you happy. But, remember I have to meet with my lawyer tomorrow morning."

Once I was sedated and asleep, Lurine took off my wedding gown and dressed me in a nightgown. My husband, Lurine, and her husband took me to the hospital.

* * *

I blinked and squinted at the bright sunlight in my hospital room. A nurse entered.

"Where am I? What day is this?"

"You're in the psychiatric ward at Mercy hospital. You've been sleeping here for three days."

"How do I get out of here! Where are my clothes?"

"Stay where you are! You're not going any place. Here's your doctor now."

"Hello, Judy. I'm Dr. Brunsmere. You're going to be staying with us a while. You're a sick girl."

I couldn't believe what I was hearing. I responded incredulously, "That's not possible. I have to get my job back! I can't stay here! Stuart put me in here, didn't he? He always was jealous of my teaching job. There's a lot at stake here! That coach has to be stopped! My friends said they'd get me a lawyer."

Doctor Brunsmere replied in slow, measured tones. "There are no lawyers in here. Now I'm going to give you something to slow down your speech. Just follow my orders, and you'll get better."

"I hate you!" I shouted, and followed that, I'm told, with a string of obscenities. "How dare you smile at me that way! Can't I at least have my tape recorder?"

"That's impossible," he replied curtly. "Just go to Occupational Therapy."

A month passed. Dad had returned to Philadelphia believing I was now being well cared for in Mercy hospital. He never knew that my speech had become slurred from the medication I was receiving, that I was more frustrated, rebellious and hateful than ever. My husband made one of his infrequent visits and I reacted angrily.

"Look at me, Stuart," I shouted as I raised my nightgown, displaying my naked body. "You can do anything in here when you're supposed to be crazy. No one even notices!"

A nurse intervened and sharply reprimanded me.

"Now, Judy, that's definitely inappropriate!"

"Inappropriate? Shit, what is 'appropriate'? Making ashtrays all day? Stuart, for God's sake, get me out of here!"

An aide of Dr. Brunsmere joined the ruckus.

"Look, you'd better cut out all that crap about getting a lawyer and suing everyone. You'll be in here for life with that kind of talk. Here's my advice: get a copy of *I'm Okay, You're Okay*. Brunsmere will like that."

By then, I was willing to do anything to get out of the hospital. Stuart brought me a copy of the book, and two days later I was out of the hospital. I was at home again to apparently face a life without teaching.

In retrospect I can see that 1973 was definitely the year in which my mania first appeared. Thinking back to the phenomenal amount of reading I did for my history classes and the insights I produced on it, the amount of essay tests I graded (writing lengthy, "perceptive" comments for each), and above all the "wonderfully creative" things I did in the classroom, I realize that I was then in my early, happy stages of bipolar disorder.

I slept three hours a night, lived on chocolate-filled donuts and other junk food, gave presumptuous advice to my fellow teachers on how to teach, and did a Jewish Hora in an assembly program. I believed I analyzed the Six Day War for my students better than Walter Cronkite. If I could have continued, without falling apart physically, there is no telling where it would have led me.

But neither Stuart nor anyone else was watching out for me. I lost twenty- four pounds that year. No one cared that I wasn't sleeping enough or that the combined strain of the housework, the cooking, taking care of Jamie and the school work was too much for me. I was overloaded with my responsibilities, the real ones and the ones I created for myself. And in 1973, the fuse blew.

In those days, I didn't appreciate how important the practice of moderation should be in a person's life. When you don't know how to pace yourself you can burn out quickly. If I had then had some lithium and a little Thorazine it would have helped. But at that time, I'd never heard of a "lithium deficiency." No doctor or psychiatrist I had seen had chosen to mention these two controls for bipolar disorder. I don't know if it was out of ignorance, stubbornness, or greed; treating lithium deficiency wasn't as profitable as therapy sessions.

Stuart contributed to my deterioration. He was definitely not a supporting or a calming influence. His first priority was his job. Had he spent some of his energy helping with Jamie, or with the shopping and household chores, I could have lasted longer. But my breakdown, I believe, was inevitable because of the compulsive drive and energy I was expending. When the physical and mental capacities are affected, the illness takes over. In my case, I needed only the confrontation with my principal as a triggering mechanism.

I was ignorant of all of this in April, 1973. I was walking, running, then plunging right into an abyss. It took me nearly 25 years to climb back out, to come to grips with it, then conquer the manic conditions I had experienced.

Chapter 7

1974—THE LOST YEAR

Recently, my father and I put our heads together to try to reconstruct the year 1974. All the rest of my life had fallen into place as I was writing this book, but not that year.

"Impossible," I told myself. "I've lost a whole year. Time is a valuable commodity and any personal history has its share of signposts, events, dates and causes and effects. But not me. Not for 1974."

It was the year after my first manic attack. Did I emerge stronger? From what I concluded, apparently not. I did remember a visit to Philadelphia with Stuart and Jamie in December of '73. "Was I all right then, Daddy?" I asked.

"Yes," my father replied, "you were all right then. You were fine." He was quiet for a moment, then asked, "Wasn't that your high school class's tenth reunion?"

"That's right!" Things were beginning to come back. "It was in April, in Philadelphia." I remembered that I was a bit over-vivacious and avoided any reference to my 1973 experiences. I guess I lied, as everyone does at a class reunion. And I had a lot more to cover up than most people did. I may even have exaggerated a bit about my teaching career during the preceding ten years. Doesn't everyone exaggerate at class reunions?

With Dad's help, I recalled a visit to the home of my old high school classmate, Juli Gottlieb. "I was so hungry for friendship that I must have told her every-thing." I did remember that she was appalled at Stuart's attitude and behavior in our marriage. She even gave me a dozen or so magazines relating to the then revolutionary women's liberation movement.

I remembered that I took the magazines, but never read them because I believed Stuart's behavior and actions were for my own good, that he loved me, and that knowledge of women's liberation could jeopardize the security my marriage offered.

"Was I really all right, Daddy, after the class reunion?"

"You seemed fine, even happy," Dad answered slowly. "You even took a five-hour bus ride to Penn State to visit your brother."

"Thanks, Daddy."

When I returned to Houston later in 1974, my father told me I spent a couple of weeks at Flowermount Hospital. Apparently, Stuart found it convenient and pretty easy to commit me under Texas law. Authorities obviously based their decisions on his judgment.

I do vaguely remember that I received some shock treatments during that stay. Unfortunately, my father can't recall the reason for my being there. Stuart Stoddard probably does, but I'm not about to ask him. After all, whatever treatment I received weakened my independence and morale and made me more dependent on Stuart.

Maybe 1974 wasn't as much a lost year as I thought. I now recall two plane trips to Philadelphia, attending that class reunion, entertaining Mom for the two weeks she visited in Houston in February, and work in a department store where I received honors as "the out-standing salesperson." About the only thing missing was the satisfaction of teaching.

I went about correcting that by searching the want ads. I found an opening for four hours of morning teaching in the sixth grade of a private school. I was accepted. I was elated.

But I had failed to realize that the school was 25 miles from my home and classes began at 8:00 a.m. That meant I drove the Houston freeways in rush hour traffic while still under the influence of sleeping pills I had taken the night before. And I never had an accident. Yes, maybe 1974-1975 was a lucky time for me after all.

God watched over me and kept me alive while I was asleep driving on a Texas freeway!

Chapter 8

MANIA FOR CONVENIENCE

Stuart always gave me the feeling that I was *fat*. The happiest periods of my life occurred when I was thin. I wanted to be happy again.

The summer before I again started my part-time teaching, I began another diet. I found a reportedly successful specialist whose prescribed regimen was an entire day's food allowance consisting of four apples and half a can of special tuna he sold. He also gave me three injections a week of the urine of a pregnant woman. I can now see how ridiculous his treatment was, but at that time I went faithfully to him for two months, and did indeed lose ten pounds. I was beginning to feel more like my old self. Perhaps things would look up for me.

Then school started and I couldn't get to the doctor for the shots. Within the month my figure ballooned, 155, 160, 165, 170. My clothes were skin tight. Was it that cookie I had eaten? I couldn't begin to figure it out. I blamed myself. I must have done something wrong. But what? I dragged around thirty extra pounds not realizing that my entire metabolism had been tampered with. Pills, shots; it was a bad road to travel.

My energy sank and my sixth grade students made

mincemeat of me. They had no trouble manipulating me so they did what they wanted. I couldn't think of one innovative thing to do. I used to be one of the most creative, energetic, well-loved teachers anywhere. What had happened to me?

Every weekday morning I drove 25 miles to the school, first dropping Jamie off at a neighbor's. I barely lasted in school till noon. I would grab my coat and retreat from a dismal morning. I never ate breakfast in those days. I was trying to save calories. That was a big mistake. I was operating on empty and my brain got the signal.

At noon, I started the long drive home, knowing I was failing miserably in my beloved teaching vocation. I made it about halfway home, then spotted a restaurant. The name of it was Frank's Diet Delight. To my growling stomach, that sounded good. I went in. I was greeted by a gigantic scale at the door. "This must be the place," I mumbled to myself. Every day, no matter how much I starved myself, the scale registered 172. This was too depressing! I ate my diet lasagna, drank a glass of water and left.

I picked up Jamie and headed home. Once in the house, I would put her in her crib with paper and crayons, and, from exhaustion and a liberal dosage of prescribed sedatives slept the rest of the day, every day. Instead of drawing on the paper, my beautiful little Picasso would draw on the wall next to the crib, jumping up and down in the process. I could hear the squeaking furniture through the wall, but she never cried. She seemed to sense that I needed her to be quiet. I just lay in my crumpled bed and slept.

That's when I began dreaming of the chess set. While at Flowermount Hospital I had formed many good friendships. One was with Bess. I made a date to meet at her house for lunch when we were released. While in her lovely home, I was mesmerized by a red and black ceramic chess set. I asked her where she got it. "I made it," she replied, "while we were both at Flowermount."

That chess set was constantly on my mind. I dreamed of ways I would create one for Arthur, my brother, who liked the game.

It was simple. I would get myself readmitted to Flowermount. My last visit, as I recalled at that time, was great! I had made friends and was stimulated by all the activities. Why not repeat the experience now when my life with Stuart was so meaningless?

I launched my plan with a night of pretended insomnia. I exercised, cleaned the kitchen and tried on old clothes to check the fit. Sure enough, after five hours of this, I was beginning to feel high. My husband became alarmed and made an appointment for the next morning with my latest psychiatrist.

This was more like it! Now I was getting Stuart's attention. When we reached the doctor's office, I started doing a Jewish Hora in the waiting room. I was really hitting my stride.

After talking to me for ten minutes, the doctor handed me an envelope of little brown pills, which I stuffed in my purse.

Stuart and I went on home, and he headed out to work. But I was feeling grand and wanted something pretty with which to pamper myself. I headed for a department store and bought three new dresses. I blew our month's entire food budget, which wasn't very much.

I was prancing around in the new clothes when Stuart returned home. I don't remember the exact details, but I was readmitted to Flowermount, where conditions were not what I had anticipated. I do remember that, because I wasn't totally manic, I wasn't having fun.

Nothing was going right. I remember asking for a special diet to lose weight. However, during occupational therapy we made a delicious lunch which included homemade ice cream. But because of my diet, I wasn't allowed to eat the lunch.

I remember one patient vividly. She brought her own black satin sheets every time she came to the hospital. I wondered why, and asked. "It keeps my personality intact," she said. It makes sense to me now, but not then.

I made no friends during that hospitalization, and felt cheated. My dream hadn't come true, although I did make the chess set.

There was one bright spot. A nurse named Nanny confided that with the help of a diet doctor and regular shots she had lost thirty pounds. Before I left for home, I asked her for the doctor's name and phone number. With his help I managed to drop 25 pounds as quickly as I had gained them. I was proud of my accomplishment.

When my brother visited later that summer, I proudly presented my handmade chess set to him. But he seemed embarrassed with my gift, perhaps because I had made it while confined in a mental hospital.

I cried for my lost dream.

Chapter 9

SHERWIN THE HOSPITAL

I had returned to Houston after a traumatic month in Philadelphia. But let me begin at the beginning. In 1975-1976 I was under the care of a Dr. David Shayne and his associate, psychologist Bob Graves. They prescribed Thorazine in heavy doses, but emphasized counseling, therapy, and sleeping pills. I really don't remember all of the different pills they were giving me, but they were all ineffective in improving my psyche. I was so bored that I decided to enroll in the nursing courses at the University of Houston. I had always wanted to help people, so this new approach seemed good to me. Hadn't I lost my teaching ability? It never occurred to me at this point that maybe it was the effect of all of the pills I took that made me fail in the classroom. It is hard to teach when you are doped up all the time.

I signed up for two courses—microbiology and Texas government. (I have no idea why Texas government was needed for nursing.) I was very tired and it was hard to focus and study. I almost got a D in microbiology, but with Mr. Graves' encouragement I pulled through with a C. I thought I was doing fine.

Stuart and I talked it over and decided that our four-year-old Jamie deserved a baby brother or sister. I, for one, wanted another child. I asked Dr. Shayne what he thought about it, and he said it was fine by him. He told me the medications he had prescribed had been proven to be safe with pregnancies. I knew the Thorazine he had me taking was a drug I had used to counteract nausea when pregnant with Jamie, and look how well she had turned out!

Anyway, after five months of trying (sex with Stuart was always trying), I got pregnant. I was ecstatic. Everything went well and when I was five months along I asked Dr. Shayne's permission to take Jamie to visit my parents in Philadelphia. He said yes, and to just call him if there were any problems.

So we went to Philadelphia, and everything started off fine. I bought a whole bunch of pretty maternity clothes there, went to nearby Atlantic City and visited old friends.

Then everything went sour. I can't remember what I did or said, but Stuart claimed, via long distance phone calls, that I was high, and made an appointment for me with a psychiatrist in Philadelphia named Jack Greenspit. Stuart flew up to join me for my visit with Greenspit, who shocked me to the core when he told us that Swedish studies had proved Thorazine caused deformed babies. He then asked us the state of our marriage.

"It's rocky," Stuart told him, which was a surprise to me. I had convinced myself that we were okay. I'll never forget what happened next.

Greenspit advised an abortion. I was stunned. Who had lied to me—Shayne or Greenspit? I begged Dr. Greenspit to call Dr. Shayne and confer. To my knowledge that never happened. I tried to call Dr. Shayne several times but couldn't reach him. I couldn't take the chance of our baby being born deformed, so I reluctantly signed the necessary abortion request forms. I was at the end of my fifth month of pregnancy.

Stuart made matters worse by flying back to his job in Houston, leaving me alone in Philadelphia to have the abortion.

I really didn't expect any more or less from Stuart. I just accepted what he did as natural.

They scooted me over to a private hospital and performed the abortion. The consequences were not to impact me till much later. At that time I merely thought in terms of losing weight. Can you believe that?

I guess that, even then, I felt that I didn't deserve happiness. I"d messed up my teaching career at Armour and it had ruined my life. I didn't understand what was happening to me and I don't remember ever questioning any of it. I just kept getting up for another round. Today I claim to be a survivor. I guess I was one then, too.

When the impact of the abortion finally hit me, I became hysterical and was whisked over to a swanky private psychiatric hospital, the Quaker Institute. This hospital had a pool, mahogany furniture, silverware and menus. At least that's what the patients who were not too sick enjoyed. My father said there were other floors where the amenities were another story. My mother and father visited me, but where was my husband? I went to a hairdresser outside the hospital and wore all of my own clothes rather than hospital gowns. Because the cases that were bad off were isolated from me, there were no adverse, stimulating influences. I made an ashtray there that I have remembered ever since. It had Reinhold Niebuhr's moving serenity prayer on it:

"God grant me the serenity to change the things I can,
"The courage to accept the things I cannot change, and
"The wisdom to know the difference."

There was no group therapy or psychotherapy for me this time. No one helped me to come to terms with the loss of my baby or my teaching career. I was not prepared to return to a life in Houston with a husband I now subconsciously hated. I was discharged from the hospital and even found the strength to return to the stores the maternity clothes I had bought. That really upset me. Above all, I needed a lot of love and understanding—understanding of my feelings, actions, and my illness. Stuart either didn't care enough to try or just found it too difficult for his range of thinking.

My parents reluctantly put me on a plane and sent me back to Houston. I sat next to a very kind man during the trip. I was holding his hand for dear life by the time we landed. He later phoned me in Houston to see how I was. This flight was a brief escape from my strange life.

Back in Houston, I was downright hostile toward Dr. Shayne. I actually refused to see him! I held the abortion against him. I still didn't understand what I had been doing in Philadelphia that could be classified as manic.

Anyway, Stuart resourcefully found a new psychiatrist named James Darring. This gave me new hope and a new chance to tell my story as best as I understood it. James Darring's program was pill free. You were just supposed to get yourself out of an inappropriate mood by repeating, "I will be calm, I will be calm." We would shoot the bull during our sessions and it would be fun. But it didn't help me conquer my boredom, or find a job, or most of all, to *sleep*. Just chanting that I felt at peace didn't make it so. My body and mind were working on high. I was quietly entering a deep mania. I was frustrated by lack of intellectual stimulation and challenge.

Then one night, I couldn't sleep at all. I had no Thorazine to take so I just stayed awake. Boy, was I bored! I took a whole bunch of old snapshots and put captions on them. That's how desperate I was. By four o'clock in the morning I was really desperate. There's nothing worse than insomnia with nothing to do. I had to get out of the house and away from Stuart.

When he finally awoke and saw that I had been up all night, he became alarmed and thought I'd better go to the hospital. It sounded like a great idea to me. Flowermount had been a lot of fun. The Quaker Institute had been nice. And best of all, my father promised to come to Houston to take care of me. I was very calm as I packed a bag, woke Jamie and reassured her that it was nothing serious. I remember the ride to Sherman Hospital. James Darring had said he could no longer treat me and I never heard from him again, so I wasn't too sure who would be my doctor. The bracelet they put on me said Dr. Al Coty.

Oddly enough, I didn't see him until I was discharged six weeks later. I could see at once that this was going to be fun.

Sherwin the Hospital, Sherwin the Park, Sherwin the Zoo. Of all the hospitals I have been in, before or since, I can easily say that Sherwin was my favorite. I spent eight of the happiest weeks of my first marriage there. It was a teaching hospital and many of the staff were in training. Psychology students from a nearby university would come to the ward and work with the patients. There was plenty of care and attention.

As in all the other hospitals, they decided at once that in my manic state I was too much of a distraction to be around the other patients. So again I was escorted to lockup. But this was no cell. It was a spacious room with a big window having a view of the city. Of course, the wood door was locked but it was ideally suited for banging on with my shoes, which they had at first allowed me to keep. I used my hands for my initial pounding, but that hurt, so I switched to using my shoes.

Naturally, after an hour of this noise, my shoes were also taken from me. There was a small glass window in the door. I was extremely happy, but wanted to complete my happiness by sharing. The best way to do this, I thought, was to sing with gusto at the top of my lungs. I chose songs with a message—my message. I sang "People," "Everything's Coming up Roses," "Don't Rain On My Parade," and "For Once In a Lifetime." For my finale I would do "Hava Nagila," and I would form my own circle for the dance. None of this exhausted me—in fact I felt increasingly exhilarated. I really don't remember sleeping very much, but when I did sleep I dreamed I could fly without an airplane.

I had the secret. My seclusion and solitude were constantly interrupted by staff members giving me shots and bringing the cosmetics which I kept demanding. I still was wearing my own clothes, not hospital gowns. There was a bathroom with a tub in the room, but the door was kept locked. The nurse would let me take a bath every so often, but I hated it because the water was allowed to drain from the tub as fast as it came in. I guess that was to prevent suicide by drowning.

I remember thinking of so many things that I decided to start keeping a diary. But nobody would give me a pencil and paper. Using great cunning, I kept my lipstick to write with. The walls of my room became my tablet, and I outlined my innovative thought. "God Loves Laughter;" "God Loves Music;" "What The World Needs Is One Song It Can Sing;" "Ask Not What Your Country Can Do For You, But What You Can Do For Your Country;" "Some Men See Things As They Are And Say Why? I See Things That Never Were And Say Why Not?"

The staff members really blew their collective stacks when they saw the red lipstick on the walls in the morning light. Of course they said I would have to pay to have the room repainted. Brazenly, I said, "Yes, and while you're at it why not make it lavender instead of this flat white?"

The general reply was, "Of all the nerve!"

That night I managed to sleep a few hours, but I again dreamed, and it seemed real to me. God was speaking to me and giving me His message, "Do not let being alone upset you. Keep your chin up. You can be happy with just ME for company. I am proud of you for your spirit and strength. I am glad that seclusion and isolation have not destroyed you. It's like a test in all of these isolation cells. I want you to see that at all of these times you must appreciate life, any kind of life that presents itself. Just remember, it could always be worse. Remember that you are a teacher. Remember the Nazi concentration camps." I woke up shouting, "I have a dream, I have been to the mountaintop!"

I was beginning to feel at home in that room. The days went quickly. The other patients became my friends. They would come to the window in the door, wave and talk to me. Although my condition was not improving, I was transferred from my security room to a regular room. Another patient, a Mrs. Sanchez, was diagnosed as worse off than I and they needed the security room for her.

I finally met Mrs. Sanchez, a wild-appearing and acting woman with long, disheveled black hair. She tried to steal my cosmetics time and time again. The nurses were frustrated, and suggested they might have to lock up my cosmetics permanently. I pleaded with them not to. Intuitively, I knew that this woman was not a thief. She just wanted to try to be pretty again. She was desperately trying to improve her appearance. We understood each other.

For the next two weeks, Mrs. Sanchez and I switched off on the lockup room, depending on which one of us was making the most disturbance. I have no idea why they just didn't sedate me to shut me up. Maybe they did and I don't remember.

When my behavior improved, I was transferred to a ward. Here, I had a ball. The day was full of activity.

I made a zodiac ashtray in Occupational Therapy. I played volleyball in a nearby gym. Every Wednesday night we saw great movies, such as "Brian's Song." And there was plenty of freshly popped popcorn. My father and daughter came every day to visit me. I was happy to see them, but it reminded me of my lost baby and I talked continuously about "Jamie Small" (as opposed to my four-year-old Jamie). I was allowed, in the custody of my father, to go out of the hospital to Sherwin Park across the street. My father's cheerful face and my daughter's presence were wonderful therapy.

They then transferred me into a private room, and this continued my improvement. I remember Stuart occasionally coming to visit me during my days in lockup. He would invariably raise the topic of divorce and I would explode. The myth of my marriage was all I had to hold on to. Throwing him out was my answer to his talk. But as I improved he became much more amiable. I guess he remembered my cooking and ironing his shirts.

While in this hospital I took an interest in my fellow patients. Here was a chance to prove that I was needed. There was one patient whose thing was cooking. She was the most fantastic cook and baker I ever met. She made pecan squares that were heavenly. There was a kitchen in the ward for just such an artist. Now, all we needed were pecans. My poor father was besieged with daily requests from the two of us and he complied willingly. We ate pecan squares till they came out of our ears. My only regret is that I never got the recipe from her.

Another patient I met was a 26-year-old girl named Jean. She was suffering from severe depression. She was sloppily overweight, had stringy, dirty blonde hair, wore no makeup and dressed in shabby clothes. We became friends and I conceived a plan. I resented her husband, who openly neglected her. I decided that I would work to improve her appearance, and that lifted her spirits. I washed her hair, styled it and then I completely changed her facial appearance with my cosmetics.

I dressed her in my hot pink outfit that was then too big for me. The product of my efforts was phenomenal. She actually was pretty. She smiled when she saw her image in the mirror. She started dieting and lost ten pounds. Her husband became very attentive to this new person, and, shortly after, they could be mistaken for honeymooners.

On the other hand, Stuart never stopped nagging me long enough to appreciate my new size twelve figure and the clothes I had bought in Philadelphia. He never appreciated all the effort I put into trying to make myself semi-attractive.

My "cure" had worked for Jean. But sadly, Mrs. Sanchez's case was not as happy. She was an aristocratic Spanish woman from a wealthy family. When she had become manic, the family considered it both a shame and an insult to the family honor. Her husband never came to the ward. Occasionally a handsome, 20-year-old son would visit. There were rumors that she was being transferred to a hospital for the chronically ill near the Texas-Mexican border.

One day they took her away. I never learned where. She just vanished. One thing I knew. She never lost her great dignity despite her illness.

My experience at Sherwin Hospital probably illustrated how empty my life was. What other explanation was there for enjoying a psychiatric ward stay so much. I realized later how fortunate I was to have been in a place like Sherwin. *But* my problems followed me and my lack of understanding of manic-depression was again to surface. These recoveries of mine were breathing spells —rest periods. I still did not understand the symptoms, the prescribed medications, and their side effects, or how to make mania work for me, if that could be possible.

Chapter 10

LITTLE HOUSE IN THE WOODS

Life went on after Sherwin. Jamie was a joy. She was a quiet, bright child who, fortunately for both Stuart and me, liked to play on her own.

I had stabilized for a while and even managed to plan and execute a birthday party for her. I loved to read to her before she went to sleep. It appeared that the worst might be over. Stuart cashed in on some stock options and made a quarter of a million dollars. I didn't interfere with how he used the money. I left it to him, and he concocted a scheme for going back to school to become a lawyer. (He was a CPA and computer expert at the time.) He insisted that only the University of Texas in Austin could meet his educational requirements. He wanted only the best for himself. As a dutiful wife, I concurred. We went through moving once again. Although Jamie had to leave her lovely school and friends, I hoped it would be a new beginning—away from mania and hospitals and such. We bid goodbye to our few friends. My psychiatrist of the week, Al Coty, wished me luck and gave me the name of his colleague in Austin.

We moved into a beautiful new home in a heavily wooded area of Austin. I could barely find the main road from the house.

I call the three years at Austin "the lost years." Dr. Zippo, my new psychiatrist, greeted me with, "How are you?" and, at Stuart's request, gave me a prescription for a strong sedative. After this it was sleep, sleep, sleep.

I did manage to pack a four course lunch every day for Stuart. Jamie insisted on peanut butter and jelly, and I was too tired to argue for better nutrition. Not that I practiced it myself. My weight was up to 160 again and I relied on Fig Newtons for my snacks. I hid them. I didn't want to fight Stuart's nagging. But he did find the package of Newtons, and, while making me watch, ground them up one by one in the garbage disposal.

I cooked meals and took care of the big house by myself. It was too much for me, sedated as I was. At this time in my life, age 32, I did not realize it was the medicine that was making me tired. I actually thought I was a *drag*.

And drag is what I did. I dragged myself out of bed at 1:30 p.m. to straighten myself to meet Jamie's bus. I always made it, though. I even managed to occasionally play a couple of games of Monopoly with her. Usually, she just watched cartoons on TV while Mommy slept. I just wasn't using my brain or common sense. I had landed in a hole and was using none of my natural resources to get out.

Finally, I took a job as a GS-1, the lowest Civil Service grade, with the Internal Revenue Service.

"It'll get you out of the house," Stuart said. "You can meet people!"

At work I filed cards alphabetically, numerically and so forth, trying to stay awake. I hoarded my small paychecks for clothes for Jamie. I paid for her after school day care out of my miniscule salary, because Stuart continued to keep a tight reign on his ridiculously slim budget.

The Internal Revenue Service is no place for someone with creativity. Besides, I was a people person, not a card shuffler.

I tried to sleep late on my days off—Saturday and Sunday. But Stuart insisted on the whole family going for day-long hikes.

He'd pull off my bed covers and announce, "We're leaving in an hour!"

I can still feel the hot sun beating down on me as I maneuvered around hillside rocks. Where was his empathy and compassion for my condition? Why didn't he notice that I was sleepwalking rather than hiking?

He loved Jamie in his own way. He called her his princess. Did that make me his queen? I think not.

I firmly believe that the depression of manic-depression was with me in Austin. But I also believe that it was mostly caused by circumstances and pills rather than a mental state.

I am basically a happy, optimistic person. I just needed a break and the right person to develop it. Stuart was not such a person. I again followed the familiar track from boredom and despondency to mania, to a mental hospital. This time it was Snail Valley in Austin. But the city didn't matter. I came to realize that too many mental hospitals were too much alike for me. The word *dehumanizing* comes to my mind.

Chapter 11

TO SLEEP, PERCHANCE TO DREAM

I remember lying motionless, almost unable to talk. This went on for almost a week. I was so very tired. Was it the medications I was on, my lost teaching career and all it meant to me, the renewed boredom of my life with Stuart, or all of these? I don't remember any activities or people during my final week in Snail Valley Hospital in Austin. There was only my roommate, Sharon LaTrec. She gave me her card, I recall, but I long ago lost it. All she wanted to do was talk. And all I wanted to do was sleep. I don't remember leaving Snail Valley, but there I was home again, in that big, isolated house.

Somehow I was at peace with myself. After all, my last siege had saved me from spending seven more boring months in a menial job with the Internal Revenue Service. So what if Stuart was giving me the silent treatment? It was spring—everything was blooming—I could see the flowers growing in my neighbor's yard. I wondered briefly why no one ever sent me flowers when I was in the hospitals; why were there never any flowers?

To my joy, most of my clothes had become too big for me. To my surprise, when I stepped on the scale, I weighed one hundred and thirty-five pounds, fifteen pounds lighter than when I had entered the hospital. This called for a celebration! I practically flew to the local ice cream parlor for an ice cream soda. I couldn't finish half of it, but it tasted so good after the hospital food.

Stuart expected me to immediately resume all my household duties and errands. He never did understand my illness and had little sympathy for me. I always tried to please him, but the more I did, the more he seemed to demand, like ironing seven long-sleeved shirts a week.

"Sure, Stuart," I complained, "doesn't it matter that I'm drugged from all the pills they sent home with me?" I see now that what I needed was some encouragement and possibly a vacation. The effects of six weeks in a hospital psychiatric ward could not be minimized, despite Stuart's efforts.

My usual room at Snail Valley was the PICU (Psychiatric Intensive Care Unit). There I yelled and screamed at the walls. I had lots of energy and creativity at the beginning of my stay, but it was all mischanneled. By the time I got out of lockup I was tired. Tired from fighting the pills and the staff. Tired from my manic high. Tired from the massive doses of sedatives shot into me. This tiredness persisted even after my return home. So, whoever said that life is easy? Certainly not me! And life is simply not a piece of cheesecake. At least it wasn't in those days.

I really dreaded Sundays. All I wanted to do was sleep. But Stuart had other ideas. I didn't understand my overwhelming tiredness and the fact that it was due to sedatives and sleeping pills. I just knew that sleeping felt good and was also an escape. But every Sunday, promptly at 9:00 a.m., Stuart would shake me and make cutting remarks:

"The house is a mess."

"You should clean more!"

"Why don't you join some organizations?"

"Can't I have more variety in my meals?"

Then he'd hit me with that zinger I mentioned earlier,

"We're going to a park to hike. Get ready!" During the week, I barely made the walk to the bus to meet Jamie. Now I was expected (commanded) to climb and hike in the hot sun. It was torture. I guess it was too much to expect him to learn from my last experience.

Stuart apparently never heard of democracies or one man, one vote. He made all the decisions. He ran all aspects of our lives. Money, clothes, food were all under his jurisdiction. The one thing he'd learned about manic people is that they tend to be reckless with money. He decided this wouldn't happen. He gave me no credit cards or checking accounts. He doled out a miserly "household fund" he expected me to stretch over two weeks. Clothes lasted many seasons. Meanwhile, Stuart, not being the financial genius he thought he was, lost heavily in the stock market.

This was a dismal period of my life. Nobody understood me or my illness. And nobody tried. Could the vegetable I had become once have been that enthusiastic, perky, dedicated teacher, Mrs. Stoddard. Something had happened to me in 1973 that I didn't understand. Nor could I understand the consequences. Nothing seemed real or relevant. Even Jamie had become merely someone to play with and care for. Dad was in Philadelphia. He came when I got sick. It seemed he never came to prevent me from getting sick.

I did want to change things but I had no idea or plan. Every month I saw a psychiatrist. He would mechanically ask, "How are you?"

I would mechanically respond, "Fine." But I wasn't fine. I was very confused. Surprisingly enough, I wasn't angry or resentful. I was just sleepy and in a dream.

Chapter 12

CHEESECAKE AS A CAUSE OF DIVORCE

If psychiatrists, psychologists and sociologists had studied Stuart's and my marriage in 1978, they could have concluded that, along with finances, religion, job pressures and in-laws, cheesecake is a major contributor to the great American divorce game. The irony is that, with the help of God, you can do something about your finances, and, of course, religion; you can change jobs; you can even try to avoid your in-laws, but what can you conceivably do about cheesecake?

By now, you should be able to guess at the setting for this incident in my life. Yes, I had just come out of a twenty-seven day stay in Snail Valley Hospital. For some reason, known only to him, Stuart was giving me the silent treatment. It was either a form of punishing me for having been in the hospital, or his guilty conscience about secretly planning to file for divorce. Who cared? I preferred the silence after my hospital bout to the nagging and bickering that Stuart usually provided.

After a week of his imposed silence, and seeing that it wasn't getting the desired reaction out of me, he switched tactics and invited me out for the evening. But this big spender's version of a night on the town was a visit to the local barbecue restaurant. Because he was too cheap to spring for a babysitter, he decided to drop eight-year-old Jamie off at acquaintances of ours, the Jamisons.

In the course of the light conversation we had when we delivered Jamie, Joe Jamison, who paradoxically was as thin as a rail, mentioned that he was a cheesecake fanatic.

"Me too," I said.

The conversation continued on the light side, with lots of laughs, oohs and aahs as Joe and I compared experiences in indulging ourselves with different kinds of cheesecake. We agreed that the worst we ever had was wonderful. It was the first time I had laughed and enjoyed myself in the seven weeks, from my last manic attack, hospital stay, and homecoming to Stuart's week of the silent treatment.

When Stuart saw me enjoying conversation with Joe, he couldn't wait to get me outside. His first words after the door closed behind us were, "God damn it, Judy, you're getting manic again. Watch it!"

"I was just having fun!" I protested. "Anything wrong with that?" Stuart drove us to the barbecue restaurant without a word.

I hate barbecue, and Stuart knew it. I guess his selection of eating fare was just another of his ways of showing his lack of feelings for me. Regardless, he ate a hearty meal, while I had practically nothing. We barely talked through dinner. When the waiter, a cheerful college student, had cleared the table, he asked if we would like some dessert. "Cheesecake's our specialty," he volunteered before we could answer.

Remembering my conversation with Joe Jamison and the fact that I really hadn't eaten much, I announced, "I'll have a piece of strawberry cheesecake."

"No she won't!" Stuart declared.

I finally had had enough, and decided to assert myself. I

looked from the waiter, who appeared surprised and embarrassed, to Stuart and said softly, "I really would like a piece of cheesecake, honey. I lost sixteen pounds in Snail Creek. Why can't I have it?"

"Because it isn't good for you!" Stuart retorted angrily.

"And all the pills I've been given are?"

Stuart ignored me, turned to the waiter and said, "We'll forget it! Check, please."

I did brush aside a tear or two, but said nothing as we drove to pick up Jamie and then back to our house. It was 8:00 p.m. I took my Thorazine and immediately fell into a deep sleep.

The next morning, Stuart woke me out of my drugged state with a ranting that also woke Jamie. "If I ever catch you eating another piece of cheesecake, I'll leave you. Do you hear me?"

My head had cleared enough for me to be indignant. Regardless of Jamie, who was standing in the doorway rubbing her sleepy eyes, her mouth open in awe of her father's outburst, I replied as calmly as I could, "Stuart, I think you're the one who's crazy. You want to leave? Go ahead and leave. You're not going to deny me a lousy piece of cheesecake."

Without a word, he took a suitcase from the closet and started packing. I had called his bluff for the first time in our marriage. In his fury, he packed an illogical selection of clothes. He attached a leash to our black and tan dachshund, Frankie, scooped up his law books and typewriter, and headed for the door. He paused briefly and announced plaintively, "Judy, I'm leaving. Do you hear? I'm leaving."

"Okay, leave!"

Dragging Frankie behind him, he slammed the door.

Jamie broke the brief silence that followed. "Mom, where is Daddy going with all his stuff? Will he come back? Doesn't he love us anymore?"

How can you answer such questions and quiet the fears of an eight-year-old? I tried. "Don't worry, Baby," I said. "Daddy was just fooling, and Mommy went along with the joke. Daddy will be back. He won't be gone for more than an hour, at most."

Fifteen minutes later, a repentant Stuart came back through the doorway lugging his suitcase, his typewriter, and books, and tugging a reluctant Frankie. "Can't we talk this over, Judy?" he asked. "You can tell I care for you."

I turned to Jamie and said, "See what I told you about Daddy, Baby? He was just fooling." It was a statement with a double meaning. He was fooling about leaving. He was also fooling about caring for me.

Chapter 13

WHEN YOU'RE AT THE END OF YOUR ROPE,
TIE A KNOT AND HANG ON

My plane landed in Philadelphia in April. My 34th birthday had been spent in lockup in Snail Valley. I didn't know it at the time, but Stuart had bought me a one-way ticket from Austin to Philadelphia. I didn't really expect a great welcoming reception, but the one I got remains unbelievable to this day. I had three hundred dollars in a savings account, with no checks or credit cards. Dad and Mom were visiting my sister Helene in Paris, France. Francis, my other sister, was busy working.

Arthur, my brother, met my plane, but looked less than ecstatic to see me. Mom and Dad's McKinley Street home looked exactly as I remembered it, which was somewhat reassuring. The next morning, Arthur left for work and I was on my own. I faced my old enemy, boredom. "Hey," I said to myself, "this was supposed to be a pleasure trip."

That night I suggested to my brother that we take a trip to Las Vegas or somewhere else. Somewhere warm. Like we used to do in the good old days when he spent every summer with us. He declined my invitation. He said he had to work. He couldn't take any leave. Where had I heard that before? That's when I started the phone calls.

"Hello, University of Pennsylvania? I need to speak to the Registrar. Yes, I want to apply for a job. I don't care, any job. Well *teaching* of course—what do you think I am, a janitor? A Bachelor's degree, but I could go for a Master's in something or other at night. I don't *intend* to fill out an ordinary application like everyone else. I'm *not* like everyone else!"

I thought I was doing something positive, but actually I was beginning a manic spiral and was getting bored and frustrated with life in general.

By then, people I phoned were just hanging up on me, including my mother-in-law, my youngest sister, Francis, and one of my former high school history teachers. I told Francis, somewhat abruptly, that her Ph.D. wasn't worth the paper it was printed on. I don't know why I said that. My unhappiness made me vicious. But it ended with her removing her phone from the hook. Francis just wasn't up to dealing with me. I had alienated a person who might have helped me.

My next idea was to get my needed vacation in Paris with my wonderful father. I phoned my sister, Helene, and she coldly told me to go back to Stuart in Austin. She said she'd have me locked up if I set foot on French soil. She began screening my parents' calls. I considered my next move both practical and realistic. I called the French Ministry to see if Helene could carry out her threats. In a word, the answer was, "Yes."

But I kept calling France, maybe a dozen times. And Helene kept hanging up, which always made me nervous.

By the next night, I was talking a blue streak. Arthur and I were in his tiny room. I wasn't at all sleepy. I was kind of exhilarated, and kept expounding on a wide range of topics, which I was sure was grating on his nerves.

Suddenly, he got a wild look in his eyes, grabbed a pillow and pushed it on my face. The pillow, with his two hundred odd pounds behind it, was beginning to cut off my air supply.

"Shut the hell up!" he screamed. "Can't you keep quiet, you shit?"

For a second I remembered my father once saying to me during one of my previous manic outbursts, "If you don't cut this out you won't live to be thirty-five." Was that coming true? In the clear section of my mind I realized I was being smothered. The pillow was pressing harder and harder on my nose and throat. I was near panic. I realized I might die right there without ever having started to live.

But I did manage to get a small gasp of air and mumbled, "I'm sorry." Arthur's body relaxed and he released me immediately. Shaken, he left.

I called the police. They thought I was a crank. Some vacation this had turned out to be.

There was very little food in the house, but I wasn't hungry anyway. I stayed clear of my brother. My life was really cratering. Where was Daddy? He could always calm me down. His patience with me was endless.

The next two days were a blur. I found out later that I had run up a seven-hundred-dollar phone bill. I think the telephone company later took pity on my father's story about it and cancelled part of the bill.

My mother and father arrived home. My Aunt Rose and her husband, Uncle Phil, visited to welcome them back. My brother announced to this gathering in our living room that I needed to go into a hospital and grabbed my arm to punctuate his statement. Aunt Rose and Uncle Phil were obviously embarrassed. They tried to treat Arthur's statement as a joke, but Arthur would have no chit chat. "You're going to a hospital where you belong," he said to me menacingly. "Come on."

I just wasn't up to another scene. "Okay, Arthur," I said.

They got Al Padget, our neighbor, to drive. As we were leaving the house I started mumbling, "Let's get this over with. Some vacation, some beach. Who am I hurting? Am I violent? I'm not suicidal or homicidal. Why do I have to go to another snake pit? Haven't I suffered enough? Couldn't I just finish my iced tea and sandwich? The food in hospitals stinks."

Arthur heard that. "No sandwich," he said, "let's go."

Then began the most bizarre ride of my life. We drove all over Philadelphia looking for a psychiatric hospital with little ol' insane me giving directions and talking to police stationed at the various hospitals we visited in Arthur's search for one that would admit me without a doctor's orders.

Finally, nearing the end of my fellow passengers' patience, we pulled into the welfare hospital. Arthur handed me over to Admitting and left. I was taken to Intensive Care where the smell of stale urine was nauseating. Bars were on the windows. People were screaming. "Is this the only hospital in town?" I asked brazenly.

My father arrived the next day with my clothes. "She won't be needing these," a nurse sneered. No group therapy in this place. It was one-to-one, whatever that meant. My one-to-one was a black-haired sexy-looking aide who worked nights as a waitress. She was tired and had little time for me. My psychiatrist was a resident, and she surpassed all the others for stupidity. She asked me what was the dumbest question anyone had ever asked me, "How did it feel in your mother's womb?"

"Warm and wet," I replied without blinking an eye.

This particular hospital was a revelation for me. Though I had, at previous times, entertained the thought that some hospitals could be *fun,* this place forever ended that myth for me.

I was almost constantly sedated during my three-week stay. I tried to borrow a quarter to phone Jamie, but when I did get through, Stuart would hang up without a word.

Daddy smuggled palatable food to me at every opportunity. It tasted so good. Then one day Daddy entered, his eyes, his face, his whole body totally serious.

"Stuart has filed for divorce," he said flatly, "and he'll get to keep all the money you should have."

There's nothing like bad news when you're in a mental hospital. I mean, what can you do except make another ash tray?

I listened calmly as my father gave me all the details, then I said, "No, he won't get away with that. I'll get out of here and I'll fight him"

Daddy still looked worried, as if his confidence in me had been undermined.

I immediately turned into the ideal patient. I willingly made my bed, was reserved, drew lots of pictures in Occupational Therapy and best of all, played volleyball in Recreational Therapy. I took whatever medications were offered and tried to remain normal in spite of their adverse effects. Had I learned any lessons? I think I had. How to play the game. That's what I learned. Also, I learned that if I was really good they would give me my lipstick. It's really hard for a woman to maintain her dignity when wearing a hospital gown and being deprived of cosmetics.

So I was out of there and on my way back to Texas with my loyal father for company. Next step would be to confront Stuart. Again my clothes were falling off of me. It must have been the gourmet lean cuisine they served in that hospital. Well, Stuart always had been nagging me to lose weight. I hoped this would satisfy him.

Chapter 14

I'M READY TO RUN
(But Ran Into Lockup, a Recollection)

"I'm a good person who is trying to be a better one!" The year was 1980. The location was my cell in the welfare hospital in Philadelphia.

My drug-induced dream seemed so real that it startled me out of my deep sleep. I jumped up to the side of my bed. I now knew all the things that had to be done to save the country, and I, as President, was going to do them. Now! In this election year. If I could only find a pencil and paper to write my ideas down.

But they would not let me have any pencil or paper. I really believed, at that moment, that I had the magic formula for saving the United States from all known and unknown problems. How could I get my words and thoughts recorded? How to get the ideas down before the vision I knew God had given me would fade? They were beginning to fade already. An urgency overtook me.

I ran around in circles inside my cell, screaming, "I must become the president. I must save the country— 'Ask not what your country can do for you, but what you can do for your country.' I, too, have a dream. I, too, have been to the mountain top". Those paraphrases sounded familiar to me. Where had I heard them before?

I was only thirty-four years old. To be president, I knew you had to be thirty-five. The primaries were beginning. "It will be too late." But the commotion I was now causing brought the attendants. One was a six-foot, three-hundred-pound man, the other a wispy grey-haired female aide with the familiar Thorazine-filled needle in her hand.

Without regard for my dignity, the male attendant threw me down on the mattress and pulled up my hospital gown. The nurse jabbed the needle into my buttock. I had never felt such excruciating pain. The dream faded. The goal of leading the nation faded. I had become a "good patient" again by hospital standards. I was asleep.

* * *

Lockups in all psychiatric hospitals are frighteningly, disgustingly the same. When the door shuts and you're all alone, when there's only a stained and torn mattress on the floor, and when you scream and no one comes, you know you're in lockup. It's scary—that feeling of being cut off from the world.

Lockup was used to punish me for loud, happy behavior in the ward. Happiness does not sit well in a psychiatric ward. I was considered a troublemaker.

The days and nights are long when you are isolated in lockup. It was solely up to me to prevent it from destroying my body and spirit. Because you're usually loaded with dope, it's not easy. Because you're treated like an animal (no toilet, for example) it's definitely not easy. I fought for my life and any remaining sanity in those places. I resisted sleeping for fear that's all I would do. There was nothing to read, nothing to write with. The boredom was killing. The only thing that saved me was my singing. I bombarded those beyond my cell walls with every possible loud, happy song I could resurrect from my tortured memory.

I guess I won, because I'm free now and can go

where I want, sing what I want and use a toilet when I want.

Most of my time in hospitals was either spent in lockup or in recuperating from the effects of lockup. I was tired out from all that singing.

I never would have made it through all those long months if it hadn't been for my belief that someone was watching over me, that someone was listening to my music, that someone was laughing at me and with me.

When I awoke, I had forgotten my dream of running for president. But I remained fully aware of being confined in a cell in the Philadelphia welfare hospital.

I kept blasting out the song, "Don't Rain on My Parade!" at the top of my lungs. I started banging on the wooden door. That was the only way I knew how to communicate with my captors. "Let me out of here! Do you hear me? You're all a bunch of Nazis!"—the image of Nazi Germany had often affected my thinking. The aide entered with my tray.

The aide put the tray on the floor since the mattress was the only item of furniture in the cell. She looked at me suspiciously and said, "Judy, here's your dinner. Eat it, and don't make a mess."

It smelled vile to me and I judged from its appearance that it probably tasted worse. "For God's sake, it's sausage. Didn't I tell you that I'm Jewish and that I keep Kosher?" For the record, I have never observed the Jewish dietary laws, but it was a game by now.

"Judy," the aide coaxed me, "can't you be a good patient?"

I picked at the food. "What is this crap anyway? Can't we get something good to eat around this place?"

"Never mind," the aide snapped. "Do you think we give out menus around here? Just eat it and hurry it up. It's good."

I felt very naughty and I deeply resented being locked up. "If the food's so good, then you eat it! Have some potatoes and take some sausage!" I threw the plate of morsels in her face.

"That was definitely inappropriate," the aide shouted in her fury, "You know what that means, don't you?"

I soon found out, as half a dozen male attendants appeared, one with a long needle.

"No, no, please," I begged them. "I'll be good. I'm sorry. I promise I won't ever do it again. But please, not the needle. Don't put me to sleep again!"

"Get down on the mattress," one attendant snarled, "and shut up."

"Please, God, no! Don't touch me!" I screamed. "I'll make you pay for this!" Of course, they won out, despite my kicking and fighting. They gave me a massive dose of Thorazine. The last thing I remember was mumbling, "Don't rain on my parade." No one paid any attention to me.

George Washington
Father Of His Country...

Judy K. Feder
Mother Of Her Country...

Feder Is Better!

Judy K. Feder
Needs You!

America Needs You!

Chapter 15

I'M GOD'S MESSENGER

During the times when I was out of hospitals I would attempt to lead a normal life. This was certainly not easy, for I didn't understand my illness or the repercussions it was causing for me. I was usually heavily dosed with Thorazine and was therefore susceptible to the dreams, nightmares and visions that drug causes. They frightened me. A lot of the time I found it difficult to differentiate dreams from reality.

When Dad and I returned from the welfare hospital in Philadelphia to Austin in 1980, I had a very disturbing mind set. I tried to relate it to my father. "Daddy," I said, "I heard God's voice again. He told me that I was His messenger. (First I was to be president, and now God's messenger.) Daddy, I heard Him! Is it my mission to save the world from the terrible state that it's in? Maybe that's why I've suffered so much. To strengthen me. God hasn't told me yet how I'll do it, but I know He will. I must start on my path. Let's go see the Orthodox Rabbi at the Chevrah House. I know he will help me."

My father grimaced, which told me without words that he was worried. He looked at me sadly and asked, "Are you sure?"

"Yes," I assured him. "I'm positive I heard God's voice."

Dad agreed to drive me to the Rabbi. The Chevrah House was the center of fundamentalist Jewry in Austin. We went in. The Rabbi was a slight, young man, though he appeared ancient and wise with his stark black garb, long, trimmed beard and sidelocks.

The Rabbi greeted me warmly and then asked how he could help me. I told him abruptly that I was the Messiah. This didn't sit very well with him.

"Young lady," he said, "you couldn't possibly be the Messiah." He then went on to educate me on the reasons that I was mistaken. "You are a female," he blurted, "the Messiah will be a male. You do not have a beard. I seriously doubt if you observe the 613 precepts. You couldn't possibly be the Messiah." If I'd had any sense of humor left I would have laughed. What a male chauvinist he was. But I sat still and said nothing.

"I'm sure you are a good Jew," he said as he rose from his chair. "Why won't you just settle for being a better one?" With that comment he left the room. The interview had ended, but not my conviction that God had repeatedly, forcefully, through my dreams, given me His message to deliver to the peoples of the world.

The Recurring Dream

For the 23 years prior to recovering from a coma (which I will tell about later), I had a recurring dream. It was of God directing me to deliver a message for Him. The dream was, no doubt, a product of my faith in God. But regardless of what some people may think, I believed its possible source and significance required me to act on it by passing it on to as many people as possible. In doing so I must emphasize that I did not believe that I had any special attributes for the mission, but was simply a messenger. You could accept the message and act accordingly. You could ignore it if you were faithless and wished to risk the consequences. Part of my dream was that God had given humankind the power of choice and wanted to see what we would do with it.

My recurrent dream was that God is so appalled and disgusted by what we have done on and to His beloved planet Earth that He is extremely angry. He therefore will no longer speak directly to humankind as He did to and through prophets and others in the past. Instead, He selected me as His sole and final messenger. Because he loves Earth and its people He first tried to warn us by increasing the number and severity of His "calling card" warnings—severe blizzards and frosts, floods, hurricanes, tornados, wars, droughts, famines, and the AIDS epidemic. ("There have been more weather-related disasters in the past five years than in all the thirty preceeding them."— President Clinton, 1997). God told me, in my dreams, that these calling card warnings have been token preludes of what He plans to unleash if humankind doesn't change from its greedy ways.

In my earliest dreams I had the effrontery to question God as to why He was selecting me as His messenger for such an unbelievably tremendous, controversial, and complex task— there are so many others better qualified in so many ways. He responded with these reasons that well could have been my delusional rationalizations:

—He saw me dedicate myself to becoming educated in teaching and problem solving through demanding post-graduate studies.

—He saw me mature into a commended, effective classroom teacher of world history, and approved my emphasis on the benefits of questioning and analysis ever since.

—He appreciated that my idealism had me believing that there remains hope for Earth and mankind.

—He appreciates that I continued to love Him with all my heart and soul, and never doubt Him.

—He knows that His Ten Commandments have guided

and always will guide my life.

—He has seen me as one of the too few people who express concern for what humankind is doing to itself and Earth, one who could anticipate the ultimate disaster God will visit upon us as a consequence of continuing our greed.

God expressed to me in my dreams that the reasons He gave qualified me to communicate His briefest message to humankind:

"I am a loving God. I am a forgiving God.
But enough is enough."

Now, as I lead what is considered a normal life, I look back on this experience and wonder if my dreams of God appointing me as His messenger were totally manic delusions? Or could there be a remote possibility that He found my manic mind a suitable receptacle for communicating His message? It's impossible to tell. But voicing, or even personally over-reflecting on this to others could definitely jeopardize the freedom I am now enjoying. The tenets of organized religions, and even atheistic beliefs that control our lives cannot tolerate the remotest possibility of the validity of such occurrences as I just described. But what about the following article, which was rejected for publication by magazines of several different religious and secular groups?

The Attributes of a Messiah
by Judy K. Feder

Christians await the return of their Messiah, Jesus. Jews await a Messiah they believe has yet to come. And what might the one God in whom both Jews and Christians (and Moslems and many others) be thinking about providing humanity with— either in a first or second coming? Let us also think about this: Because God made us in His own image, we may well attribute some of humankind's thinking and reasoning processes to Him. If this is so—

God will consider how well we will pay attention to a new or returned Messiah. Will God's words, which the Messiah speaks, alone persuade us to discard our greed, that basic root of all troubles for humankind and its environment? Will the Messiah's words alone lead to global peace, universal love? No, I think God knows us as being too imbued with selfishness and other destructive ways for a Messiah's words alone to achieve His desired influence. So, God might ponder, should the Messiah be a paragon of action? I think not, for He will know that the laws of nature He instituted and made irrevocable provide that every action has an equal and opposite reaction.

Thus, God will be perplexed; the Messiah will not succeed as only a messenger of words, nor as only a deliverer of action. Indeed, God will have had disappointing proof of all this. Martin Luther King, a man of great heart, delivered God's words of equality and peace only to be cruelly struck down. Robert Kennedy, a man of great heart and intellect, delivered God's words of charity and hope, also only to be cruelly struck down. Jesus spoke, for the benefit of all humankind, purely and idealistically with his parables and teachings; but he also took action with the feeding of the multitudes, the curing of the leper and the cleansing of the temple, only to meet a most cruel end. It may well be that God's being perplexed as to the necessary attributes of a successful Messiah is the reason almost 2,000 years have passed without a second coming, or why the Jews have yet to welcome their Messiah's arrival.

But there is a limit beyond which God will not choose to remain perplexed or inactive, and there is a limit to His patience for the manner in which humankind has been treating His messengers. Thus, He may choose to simply dispense with His humankind creation through plagues and natural catastrophes. Or, He may choose to send a Messiah of special attributes and stand by his side, or to send a Messiah reinforced with His powers and strength.

Where we are objective we cannot consider the first

alternative unfair. We have succeeded as a species only by ignoring moral values. We have—and continue to-hurt, maim, and kill one another. We have destroyed thousands of animal and plant species and raped the very Earth with which He blessed us, all out of greed.

God would not likely choose the third alternative, for a Messiah possessing God's powers and strength would inevitably have to use these to convince us of his or her validity and of the benefits the messianic message promises. This use could well result in injuries to or death of members of humanity who scoff at and reject the message and the messenger. Those most likely to be harmed are the very persons God would most want returned to His fold.

Thus, God could find the second alternative the most promising, a Messiah having special attributes and whom He reinforces. But what might such attributes be? To conjecture, let us consider that we may now be on the threshold of the Jews' Messianic Era or the Christians' Second Coming. We do not yet know the attributes God has given His Messiah so we cannot yet identify this messenger. Is the messenger a he or a she, soft spoken and placid, or with a clarion voice and forceful? Anyone we meet may be that messenger as long as the message is one teaching us the paths we need follow for doing only good rather than evil. And it is certain that God has already given us hearts and minds that can discriminate between good and evil.

But beware, God will likely be at His messenger's side to punish those who scoff at and disobey words of goodness. Indeed, His messenger may well be already delivering the good teachings, and meeting scoffers. Are these scoffers witnessing examples of God's displeasure as inflictions upon them and theirs of epidemics and natural disasters? As He is a forgiving God, these punishments and examples could remain limited and temporary. No hurricane or typhoon has yet become a 40-day and night, global flood; and we are reported now to be nearing a cure for AIDS, an epidemic currently afflicting nearly 31 million people globally.

It must be concluded that our futures, the future of humanity, rests on our tuning in every lesson for, every admonition to do what we will recognize as good. For we know not which teacher, which speaker for good is the Messiah with God alongside.

Chapter 16

CONVERSATIONS IN TWO PARTS INCIDENTS IN SNAIL VALLEY, OR MANIA MELODRAMA

PART I
Dialogue Between Two Manics

A man about 35 with a very young face, hair dyed white, wearing makeup and nail polish. He walks over to me.

MAN: "I am Jesus Christ, my child."

JUDY: "And I am the Messiah. It's good to finally meet you. God has spoken to me and told me to spread your word."

MAN: "Then you believe in Me?"

JUDY: "Of course. Why would you lie to me?"

MAN: "They who believe in me shall come into the Kingdom of Heaven. Come unto me, all ye children that suffer."

JUDY: "I have suffered, Jesus. Help me to do the right thing."

MAN: "Would you do something for me?"

JUDY: "Of course."

MAN: "Give me that Jewish star that's around your

neck. I would treasure it. I'm Jewish, too, you know."

JUDY: (She takes the star from her neck) "Take good care of it. I've had it since the first time I went into the hospital."

MAN: "Judy, you're a beautiful person. Would you like me to polish your nails for you? Then you'll feel pretty. It helps in a place like this."

JUDY: "I'd like that."

NURSE: (Taking Judy aside) "We're putting you in Psychiatric Intensive Care Unit tonight. That Jesus character might come to your room and try to rape you."

JUDY: "How can you think that of him? He wouldn't hurt a fly. I know he won't hurt me."

NURSE: "No, it's PICU for you. Come with me for your shot."

PART II
Always A Lady

Judy is in the Snail Valley Hospital's Psychiatric Intensive Care Unit, known to the patients as PICU, or lockup. One of the mental health workers is a twenty-four-year-old named Ben. Judy has a far away look in her eyes. She is disheveled and wearing a hospital gown. She stops suddenly and turns to Ben with a sexy, provocative look on her face.

JUDY: "Don't I have a fantastic body?" She lifts her gown and says desperately, "Please, Ben, I love you. Come, let's go back in my cell and make love. I promise I won't tell anybody." Softly she adds, "I just want to be with you."

BEN: "Judy, honey, you know I really can't do anything like this. Do you know what I would really like you to do? Start dressing up more appropriately and acting more like a lady, because you have very many fine qualities. Will you please do this for me because, I really care for you."

Judy is startled. She obviously did not expect such kindness and gentleness. She listens to him.

BEN: "You have fine qualities. You're a warm, sensitive person. And you're beautiful and graceful when you take care of yourself."

JUDY: "Ben, could you teach me how to dance like a lady?"

They start to dance.

BEN: "One, two three, two, two three, three, two three." They waltz.

Judy appears to be returning to her original self and smiles at Ben happily.

JUDY: "Ben, you're one of the nicest people I've ever met. I needed this today."

BEN: "I try to be as good as I can possibly be. You must try, too. And remember, you must always be a lady."

* * *

I have never lost the feeling of shame I experience when I remember that moment when my mania overcame my moral judgement. But there is also a feeling of gratitude for the protection God extended to me through the honor, kindness and understanding he instilled in Ben. Ben had admonished me to "always be a lady." I now try so hard to do so, since he set an example for me by being such a gentleman.

Chapter 17

HOW SHOCKING!

I had been discharged from Snail Valley, but my psychiatrist, my father, and even I recognized that I was not completely recovered. So, during the period that divorce formalities were going on, my psychiatrist of the month, Dr. Carson, decided he needed to literally knock some more sense into me.

Have you ever heard of *out-patient shock treatments*? Neither had I, but I will never forget them. I don't know how many of these treatments I received, but it was definitely one too many. Maybe they used them as a last resort. They certainly represented someone's misguided attempts to improve my behavior.

The shock treatment procedure took only about half an hour. I'd arrive with Daddy at the hospital around eight o'clock in the morning. Dr. Carson would greet me. I would enter the treatment room, climb up on the table, and, since I was usually in good spirits before the fact, I would start with the bad jokes: "Dr. Carson, I am shocked at you." "Doctor, this is shocking. Please let me out of here." Ignoring me, they would then apply electro-shock therapy.

I was not joking when it was over. I'll never forget how I felt afterward. I stumbled out of the room to my waiting father.

I was not at all sure who I was or where I was. But I had a splitting headache. Of that I was positive. I couldn't put two words together. When I finally managed speech, a few whispered, garbled words came out. "Daddy, please, let's go."

Leaning heavily on my father's arm, I limped out, listening to his words of encouragement. "There, it's over. Let's get something for you to eat." My father's cure for the world's and particularly my problems was usually food. But it's the thought that counts, right?

The night before one of these treatments, I was allowed no food or liquid. I can feel the thirst I experienced till this day. Dad was always there with the shaved ice for me to suck.

Each shock treatment episode ended with breakfast at a nearby restaurant. Needless to say, my appetite usually had disappeared. But I did try to eat a little to make Daddy cheer up. After all, how much worse could things get?

I had no insurance to cover the shock treatments— or, for that matter, any other medical attention I might require—because the divorce settlement was not final. I didn't even have a checking account. Through Daddy's efforts, both Dr. Carson and the hospital billed me at welfare rates. But they still did bill me. I guess I was receiving bargain basement psychiatry. Cheaper rates but no cure.

I continued to go to Dr. Carson's office two to three times a week. It filled up some of the long days, and he constituted a captive audience for an hour. I would show off, trying to be as witty and funny as possible. The ever present box of tissues for the depressed patients was there, along with an alarm clock to turn off the manic ones. When your hour was up you were out of there. No matter if you were in the middle of a word, a real thought or even having a major breakthrough. It made me want to talk even faster than manics characteristically do. I sure wanted to get my money's worth. Looking back on it, I feel that nothing productive ever came from these sessions.

I may not have been wiser or calmer from these visits but I was certainly a lot poorer. You'd better believe that!

And my post-Snail Valley life did give me a chance to see myself as others did.

SNAIL VALLEY INCIDENT IN THIRD PERSON
Or
She Wants Her Jamie Doll

The harsh light flowed from the single lamp in the ceiling of the cell, past the protective wire mesh surrounding it to rebound off the cracked and soiled plaster walls. It cast the room into a mosaic of light and shadow. (This seemed impossible, but I was floating above myself, watching myself!) The light reflected off the grey concrete floor to highlight the other Judy's make-upless, drawn and pallid features. Her huddled form rocked back and forth at the edge of the dirty mattress lying on the floor. Her father, haggard and worn from the ordeal, sat next to her. At his side was a brown paper sack with oranges he had brought. He was peeling one of them.

The other Judy appeared to be seeking escape from the events of the past week—the possibility of divorce, confinement in a mental ward, and finally the room. She seemed to find it in the protective walls of her childhood. Mentally she was again a six-year-old. She was crying, "Please, Daddy, take me home. They won't let me have my writing tablet or my crayons." Even her voice had become thin and reedy like a six year old's. "Calm down now, Judy," Sam said as he handed her a segment of orange. "I'll be taking you home soon." "At least make them give me my Jamie doll," Judy lamented. "You can have your Jamie doll when you come home," Sam said, a tear rolling down his cheek.

"Why are you crying, Daddy?" Judy asked. "Eat your orange, Judy. It's good for you. You haven't eaten for two days."

The grinding of a key in a lock interrupted the conversation. The door of the room opened. Dr. Kinwell entered.

"Hello, Sam. Hello, Judy. How's my little girl today?"

"They won't let me have my Jamie doll, Dr. Kinwell," Judy replied, "and the food is terrible!"

"I think I know a way we can get you to where the food is better," Dr. Kinwell said. "It's nothing that will hurt you for even a moment. It's called 'shock treatment,' but for us to use it, Judy, you have to sign this paper."

"They won't give me anything to write with, Dr. Kinwell," Judy said.

"Here, use my pen," he offered.

"Are you sure shock treatment won't hurt?" she asked.

"Doctor," her father asked with concern in his voice,"Isn't it dangerous?"

Dr. Kinwell answered in a whisper, "Shock treatments are the only way left."

Judy signed the permit with a childish scrawl.Her father, a tear in his eye, reached over and wiped a drop of orange juice from Judy's chin, then stood up and took her hand, lifting her to her feet.

The three of them then left the cell.

Chapter 18

MEETING ALLEN—
A BLIND DATE, OR
BLEEDING IN THE GUTTER

The summer of 1980 was a hot one in Austin. Luckily, the apartment my father and I had rented had a couple of pools. My father loves to swim, or rather to do the "Sam stroke," which is somewhat of a poodle paddle. Knowing how little pleasure he was having, I'd get into my bathing suit and urge him to come with me. It didn't take much encouragement.

That summer with my father will always remain a fondest memory. Dad's goals were to get me well, and for me to receive a fair share of money from the divorce settlement and get a good custody agreement. We accomplished one out of the three things.

Because being well to Dad meant eating well, we did just that. We explored probably every decent restaurant in Austin, and even hit a few that were not so decent. I was on a lot of medication (hundreds of milligrams of Thorazine), visited with a psychiatrist three times a week and ventilated to him in my inimitable way.

My father worked with my lawyer and was tough as nails. He was fighting for his daughter's security and future.

Stuart was fairly agreeable about the money. Part of this could likely be attributed to him having a guilty conscience from serving his wife with divorce papers while she was in a mental hospital a thousand miles away. I'll never know.

One night, while I was particularly doped up, Stuart came to the apartment and started talking my head off. He said it would be better for Jamie if she lived with him and he had custody, that he could provide for stability and a steady job income. He then asked me to sign away my custody rights. He was so persuasive and convincing that night *and* I was so tired and depressed about my future that I signed a paper that no doubt definitely altered Jamie's life—it gave Stuart sole custody. A judge had endorsed Stuart's petition before I signed it. My hand had been shaky, but I had signed my daughter over to Stuart for what he said would be her own good. That was probably the dumbest thing I ever did.

I needed to restore my faith. My parents and I had begun to attend Friday night services at the local temple. The congregational leader, Rabbi Freeman, was a learned, soft spoken person who earned great respect from all with whom in came in contact.

One day, I got my father's okay, and drove to the synagogue to visit the Rabbi. He had a slight build and kindly eyes. I always notice a person's eyes before anything else. I told him all my troubles; about Stuart, the divorce, my illness and the hospitals.

"Rabbi, you've got to help me do something about Snail Valley's psychiatric ward. Its intensive care unit is a pest hole. The place smells. It's so dark. They kept me in seclusion in a room that had no toilet. When I had to go to the bathroom, I had to yell. No one ever came. The boredom was terrible. I was locked up for twenty-one days without anything to read or to write with. My father was my only visitor. Rabbi, I kept begging them to let me see you. But you didn't come."

Rabbi Freeman looked sad. He saw that I had obviously

been through quite a lot and he had no pat answers. He thought a moment and then put a hand on my shoulder.

"Judy, you must try to forget this. You've got to get your mind off of hospitals and such. I believe that you should go out and have a little fun. Forget the past." I looked into his eyes and saw that he was really trying to help. But how could I forget the past eight years?

"Rabbi, I don't want to forget. If things were so bad for me in Snail Valley, a private hospital costing $150 a night, they must be worse in the state institution where there are fifty beds in a ward. All that the hospital staffs do is try to keep everything under control and quiet by using sedatives." I couldn't stop myself. The words kept tumbling out. All the frustration I felt was pouring forth.

The Rabbi reached into his desk and pulled out a piece of paper which he handed to me. He explained that it was an announcement for the Austin Jewish Singles Group monthly meeting. "I've heard good things about this group," he said. "A Dr. Feder is the president. Why don't you call him?"

By this time I was losing patience. "I don't want to date," I protested. "I'm not even over my divorce yet. I just want my husband back." Right then and there I should have realized how bad off I was if I wanted Stuart back. I thanked the Rabbi politely and drove slowly home, feeling pretty discouraged. I had stuffed the announcement he had given me in my purse and quickly forgot about it. It was a paper that truly would change my life.

Later that day my mother, who was in Austin visiting, opened my purse to get some change. "What's this paper about a singles group?"

"It's nothing, Mom," I said. "Just something the Rabbi gave me."

"It looks like it might be interesting," my mother continued to prod. "Why don't you phone? Maybe it will be a chance to make new friends." My mother is very good at phoning people and talking to strangers. I'm not. If it hadn't been for her I wouldn't have called.

Dr. Feder answered the phone. He would later tell me that he wasn't a medical doctor but rather a rock doctor, with his Ph.D. in geology , geophysics and engineering. I got right to the point. "Dr. Feder," I said, strangling the phone, "my name is Judy Stoddard, I'm 34 years old, and recently separated from my husband. Rabbi Freeman told me about the singles group. Would I want the over or under thirties group?"

Allen Feder immediately answered my question by assuring me that I would definitely want the over thirties group. He just happened to be the head of it. I told him that I was sure it was nice but that the other group was having a meeting at a Mexican restaurant and that sounded like fun.

Allen was not to be denied. He suggested that he take me to his favorite Mexican restaurant, that it was as good as any he'd tried when he worked in Mexico. He described their delicacies to me and I liked his enthusiasm.

I'd like to go with you," I replied softly.

Saturday night came. I spent three hours getting ready. I saw the red car he had described stopping in my driveway. Looking out the window, I spotted a middle aged man, perhaps around 50, with a receding hairline and greying hair getting out of the car. He was wearing a cranberry print shirt and cranberry slacks with a huge, silver eagle belt buckle. I wasn't too sure about this man. I scurried into my bedroom and waited to be announced by Dad or Mother. I heard my father talking to him in the living room. I came out wearing my best pants and jersey. I had dressed to impress him.

Allen claims it was love at first sight. For me it was a chance to get out of both my apartment and eight years of hell. Allen looked happy with my appearance. "Your father gave me good directions." He smiled. "I hope you don't mind. My car has no air-conditioning."

"Don't worry about it," I replied. "It's *only* 95 degrees."

My parents seemed glad that I would have a nice time with an apparently nice man. We left and headed for the restaurant.

Later, Allen told the story differently to different people. Usually he brazenly claims that I was driving my car and that I hit him and knocked him down, bleeding in the gutter. When he came to, so he says, he opened his eyes and saw me and fell in love.

His other story—one that only partially reflects his oddball sense of humor—is that I kidnapped him away from Gypsies. Go figure.

His enthusiasm and clean features had me thinking he was just past his mid-40's. He surprised me during dinner when he told me he was 52.

I was 34, but was having a good time. The meal tasted wonderful and I finished everything—not even counting the calories.

He asked me if I'd like to have a drink. That sounded nice but, I couldn't mix alcohol with my medications. I ordered a Shirley Temple and we began to talk. I found myself telling him my whole story. This in itself should have scared him away. But he was a good listener and extremely kind in his responses. We went back to his dingy apartment, where he got out his photo albums of Iran, where he had lived for four years before escaping one jump ahead of the revolution.

I was feeling very warm and attractive. That evening Allen achieved what all my psychiatrists had failed to do. He made me feel good about myself. He made me feel pretty. For this I was very grateful, and I moved over to the couch, curled up on his lap and started kissing him. He was obviously responsive, and maybe a little flattered that a 34-year-old could have such things in mind with him. And on a first date, too.

I was starved for any kind of affection from a man. It had been a long time. It was a beautiful evening, but afterward I figured I would never see him again. I had acted like a slut and thrown myself at him. Everyone was right. Manic people are promiscuous. But still, it was nice to meet someone I could relate to.

Allen did call me again. He started courting me in earnest. He had very little money. He had made it out of Iran with nothing but his proverbial shirt *and* a bunch of souvenirs. His four children's needs siphoned off the rest of his cash, draining his resources.

We dined in ethnic restaurants because Allen loved to reminisce about all the countries he'd traveled through-and they were cheaper. No Chateaubriand for us. I didn't care a bit. All the attention I was getting was sufficient for me. We went to singles club parties and made love a lot. He proposed to me on our third date, our fourth date and so forth. He explained that the eighteen year difference in our ages did not really matter. He would always be there for me. I just couldn't believe someone could love me. I did not miraculously get normal.

I was on one of my plateaus. My body and mind were not healed by love, but it sure affected my behavior. I do not remember much of these days, however, because I still was on a lot of Thorazine. Allen later told me he thought I had a speech problem because I slurred my words all the time. I tried not to, but being over-medicated did not help me in this endeavor.

The symptoms of my mania started to return; the over-talkativeness, the flight of ideas, the delusions of grandeur, the inability to sleep. Someone decided that my old room at Snail Valley had been empty too long. I was admitted, and really bad off. I didn't even care about getting my lipstick and clothes. I just wanted rich desserts, especially cheesecake.

Allen, unbelievably, continued to court me and complied with my pleas for cakes and other contraband. He searched all over town for foods to tempt me. He must really have loved me if he could stomach the hospital and watch me behave like an animal. But they treated me like an animal, and I behaved in kind.

When I was discharged from Snail Valley, I weighed an additional ten pounds. Maybe it was the chocolate cheesecake Allen brought me daily. Just a guess. I felt terrible. I had just about had it with Austin. When Allen suggested we get married and move to Houston it sounded really good. He had gotten a new job, we would have a new wonderful life together. Jamie, living with her father in Houston, would be able to spend time with us. Best of all, Allen would take care of me. We went back to the apartment where my father was eating his usual snack of crackers and cheese. (He does love cheese; he's a real addict.) We announced our big news and Allen formally asked for my hand. I don't know what my father's thoughts were. He genuinely liked and respected Allen. Maybe he was just a little relieved that some of the burden would be off his shoulders, but he would never say anything like that. He had been carrying the load for a long time. He must have missed his home and friends in Philadelphia, although he never mentioned it.

As far as I was concerned, I've always been a practical person. I could see clearly that my future without Allen was bleak. I was on the way to self-destruction. I couldn't even remember the names of all my psychiatrists. I was doped up, and sluggish. Allen said it would be a fresh start. A new life. A new deal. A square deal. A fair deal. I had come out of the divorce with a settlement of $70,000. When I had mentioned it to my aunt she had sneered, "At the rate you're going, you'll waste it on hospitals in no time."

I decided that things would be better for everyone if I went ahead and married Allen. Maybe he was a dreamer, but he was opening a new world for me. My life had been disastrous for so long I was willing to try anything—even marriage. It was either Houston with Allen or Philadelphia with its bad memories.

I chose Houston. I wanted desperately to believe that with Allen I could beat the overwhelming odds against me.

Only time would tell.

I'll tell you more about Allen in chapter 27.

Chapter 19

SAM

Because of what I have written before, and what is still to come, I must give you more details about an exceptional man.

Sam, my father, and I have been through a lot together, and there exists a special love and bond between us that will never be severed. Sam has loved me, worried about me, encouraged me, cared for me and administered to me in my illness episodes, made me smile when I didn't feel like it, aided me in my work, and fed me.

I emphasize feeding because when I was losing much weight each time I went into a hospital, he would bring me lox on a bagel, or a corned beef special. His soft boiled egg, tea and toast each morning would get me ready for a tough day at school. He really is sold on good nutrition and is an avid reader on the subject.

I sometimes kid Sam about the two of us being the "Bobsey Twins," and I guess our theme song these last few years might be from *Gypsy*, "Together, Wherever We Go."

Sam is not only a great father, he is a friend. He and Allen are my best friends. Sam stuck by me when I was not easy to be with, a victim of my ranting delusions and insults during my manic attacks.

Dad never seems to want anything for himself. Clothes, cars, houses and other material things mean nothing to him. He really takes life a day at a time. He would give me everything he has, anything I wanted; he would fulfill my every material need if I would let him.

Allen rapidly grew to love him as I do. We particularly enjoy his ability to thoroughly savor a good meal, mopping up the dressing from his Greek salad and entree gravy with his bread. He'll never admit that he's full after a hearty meal, always merely "comfortable." My father also was a wonderful husband. When he visited us alone, in Houston, he phoned mother in Philadelphia three times a day; and he scavenged every newspaper for coupons to aid her shopping and charities.

When Sam, as a teacher's aide, was giving me material and moral support in my classroom, he developed a wonderful relationship with my students. Out of love, rather than disrespect, they too were calling him "Dad," as I did.

Today, at ninety, Sam attests to his youthfulness by bicycling to the post office daily, or to the grocery store, the library, or just touring the neighborhood. He goes to bed at 10:30 p.m. and wakes at 5:15 a.m., before any alarm in the house sounds. He occasionally catnaps in the early evening after a particularly hard day, but for the most part keeps going on snacks of crackers and cheese. (He relishes a good Brie cheese as much as a Chateaubriand.) All that at ninety.

My father's favorite—perhaps his only—TV show is "Wall Street Week." He had deep interest in what he sees and hears, and can quote from the program much as he can from the business section of the daily newspapers. You would never guess that he didn't own a single share of stock.

Sam never goes anywhere without his shirt collar buttoned, and his necktie properly knotted. I kidded him that I'd seen him wear a tie to bed with his pajamas.

Sometimes I think the doggy bag was invented for my father. He loves to bring home leavings from our restaurant meals. He is not greedy—he's the most generous and sharing person I've ever met. He is not a glutton—he's actually unhappy if those he's dining with won't share from the dishes he's enjoying, and he enjoys so many. It's as though he wants to prolong the pleasantry he finds in dining with friends and family by putting it in the doggy bags with the food. As a consequence, when he visits with us, our refrigerator and freezer will be bursting with small foil and Saran wrapped packages containing thirds of steaks, half bowls of onion soup, quarter pieces of pie, and a variety of breads, rolls and muffins that would do a bakery proud.

Perhaps related to Sam's doggy bag syndrome is the fact that he's a collector. He collects paper bags, plastic containers and utensils, glass jars of every shape and size, newspapers, rubber bands, and pieces of aluminum foil and Saran Wrap. Allen and I love Sam, so it wrenches our hearts when he ends a visit with us and we must clean out the dozens of things that he has collected and saved for us out of love. We must admit, however, that when Sam is with us, we never lack for just that right item to store, bind, or throw away in proper style.

I could tell of his common sense philosophy and a host of other reasons why I love him. But I'll sum it all up by saying that I love him for just being what he is. I'm so lucky to have him for a father. My life would have been so totally different, so negative, if he hadn't been with me.

Allen loves conversing with my dad. They have much in common, such as world interests and technical background. (Sam is a retired aeronautical engineer and Allen is an earth and space scientist and engineer.) But Allen relaxes by writing technical articles, and of all things, poetry. I tell you of this now to introduce Allen's birthday tribute to this man we both love so much.

SAM KANISS, FINE: VINTAGE '07
  The gods in the heavens,
  (Oh, how they shine),
  Wished to toast one another
  With the finest wine:
  —Chose Vintage '07
  Of *Sam Kaniss, Fine*.

  "'Tis robust," shouted one;
  "Most mellow," all agreed.
  "It sparkles." "It's fun."
  —"A classic, indeed."

  "A pleasure to behold."
  "A blessing, most rare."
  "Of all the wines sold,
  None can compare."

  "It has humor," said Zeus,
  Father of all,
  "Tang and spice, mellow youth,"
  Downing glass tall.

  "We chose well, indeed,
  In bringing forth such a wine,
  To fill the earth's need,
  Sam Kaniss, Fine."

  Love,
  Signed Allen
  August 18, 1987

Chapter 20

PROMISES, PROMISES

On November 23, 1980, I passed a definite milestone in my life. That's the day I "stumbled" down the aisle and married Allen Feder. I say "stumbled" because I had on a pair of cheap, dyed, high heeled shoes and could barely walk. There was also mental stumbling involved, because I was groping around to find a new life to replace the tragic or near tragic old one I longed to leave behind.

It was to be a good decision. Marrying Allen turned out to be a wonderful idea, as you will see. I always say that God sent Allen to take care of me. My father was tired, and I needed someone. I couldn't take care of myself in those days.

Our wedding was something that just happened. I had no control over my life in those days, and my wedding was no exception. If I had it to do over I would have been married in a white gown in Philadelphia with all our relatives present. I would have had flowers in my hair. There would have been a honeymoon. Oh, what the heck, don't I have enough dreams?

Actually, it was a nice little wedding. Allen looked handsome in the new suit, tie, shirt and shoes I had bought for him. Remember? I had received $70,000.00 from the property settlement with Stuart thanks to my father's perseverance, the determination of our very nice lawyer, and Texas property settlement laws. My lawyer disliked Stuart for divorcing me while I was in a hospital. He called it "dirty pool." That much money is not to be sneezed at, and I felt a new security.

We videotaped the wedding and reception. It was a new technique then. I think the tape is "lost" somewhere in Dad's house in Philadelphia. I'd like to see it again to learn all about my second marriage. I wonder what I did while participating in such a momentous event.

My brother Arthur and my sister Francis flew in from Philadelphia for the ceremony. I bought a new size fourteen dress, which was all right but not great. Daddy looked downright noble in the new suit I bought for him. To this day it is still his best suit. Jamie was dressed up, but felt a little queasy. She assured me it wasn't because I was getting remarried. She liked Allen from the beginning. When the photographer asked how long she knew the bride, she replied, "Practically all my life." I loved it.

Altogether there were twenty-five people at the reception. My hairdresser and her daughter were there and a couple of members from the Austin Singles Group. I always kid that there might have been one or two strangers that wandered in. I didn't quite recognize everyone.

Allen had been married 24 years in his "former life." He had some permanent scars from this liaison. Well, I had my scars, too. Some of them were pretty fresh.

When I look at the wedding pictures, I see a Thorazine insipidness in my face. But I think I can also see a look of hope and peacefulness. Everything was encouraging as we left the next day for Houston and Allen's new job. Adios, Austin. Houston held lots of memories. I planned to make some additional ones—good ones. I was justified in this expectation if for no other reason than Allen's caring, sincere and romantic nature.

Chapter 21

I DID IT WITH A LITTLE HELP FROM MY FRIENDS

A Milestone

The year was 1981. Allen and I had been married a year and a half. I was pretty content. I had money in my checking account, and Allen appreciated me. He loved my attempts to cook exotic, ethnic meals. He complimented me so much I really began to believe a little of it. I decorated our new town house, bought a lot of size twelve clothes, ate out a lot with Allen, and tried to make our marriage as good as I could.

Allen saw that I missed teaching very much, so he prepared and mailed applications for positions with a couple of the local school districts. I really don't know how he filled out those applications without my help. At least I don't remember giving him any help. But Allen is very resourceful and imaginative when it comes to resumes, and I guess he painted me in such glowing terms that no school district could do without my services.

To my great surprise, the Hawthorne School District responded with an invitation for an interview with the principal of a middle school. I was ecstatic and very grateful for this opportunity.

The principal was a straight-forward, no nonsense administrator. She offered me a sixth grade social studies position. I jumped at it. I couldn't believe it. Maybe Allen was right. Maybe, just maybe, you make your own luck and destiny.

My happiness with my new life favorably affected my mental equilibrium. I wasn't yelling at those close to me, nor was I irritable or irrational. It never entered my mind that the hidden enemy, mania, could attack at any time. I was still taking a lot of medication and was suffering some nervousness because of it.

September came. I went to in-service training at the school. The first day, after two meetings, I had an anxiety attack. I felt horrible. All the doubts came back. I couldn't function. What to do?

I somehow managed to drive home during my hour and a half lunch break (our home was only five miles from the school). I was a nervous wreck. The full impact of the job's demands closed in on me. What if I failed? This was my big chance to get my career back and work with children. The importance of this to me cannot be exaggerated.

I phoned Allen at his office. Thank God he was in. He came home and literally talked me out of my nervous state with encouragement and common sense advice. He told me to take a Valium, get something to eat and see how I felt. No pressure from Allen. By the end of the lunch hour I was able to return. No one back at the school had noticed anything strange about my behavior. I hadn't even been missed. But I realized that I was handicapped from the start.

I had to take prescribed Thorazine in order to sleep at night. By this time I was addicted to it and had to take it early enough in the evening so that its effects would wear off by 6:15 a.m. when I had to get up to be at work on time. There were too few post work, pre-sleep hours for the lesson planning and grading of papers that go hand in hand with effective teaching.

Following the status report I phoned to Sam in Philadelphia concerning the events of my first days on the job, my father instinctively realized that I needed his help in order to manage. He packed his little plaid suitcase and took the next plane to Houston. He always left a pair of his shoes and selected items of clothing with us whenever he ended his previous visits. I think he did this to reassure me that, like General Douglas MacArthur, he would return.

I was really happy to see Sam. He was seventy-six that year, but he had so much energy that he struck me as being much younger. My mother had once again encouraged him to come and help me.

He started out in the kitchen—preparing a tuna on rye and vegetable soup. I wasn't eating properly in those days, and he realized that I still wanted to be thin. And because the body is a very sensitive machine, poor eating habits were probably influencing my mental condition. Before he went to bed, no matter how tired he was, he would leave some kind of nourishing snack in the refrigerator for my nightly forays. Sometimes it would be little chunks of watermelon from which he had carefully removed the seeds. Other times it would be cantaloupe balls. His specialty was hand-squeezed, diet lemonade—three glasses waiting for me in the refrigerator. I was spoiled rotten. He must really love me a lot.

On one of my trips to Philadelphia I wanted to spoil him. I cooked several of my best dishes, bought him beautiful clothes, and picked up the tab in the restaurants. I soon realized he was not at all happy about this treatment. I now know that he prefers to give and do for those he loves, not get.

It was extremely difficult for me to get ready in the morning for school that year. In those days, I was not exactly what you'd call a morning person. The Thorazine dosage of the night before remained in my system until almost noon. With Daddy's help, however, I managed to make it through the mornings.

In the first days of the semester, Daddy just drove to the school with me for moral support. Then he started coming in to the classroom as an observer for a little while. By the end of September he was working alongside me. There was a VIP program, Volunteers in Public Schools, in my district. Daddy became a senior VIP and later won a plaque for his services.

But I was under a teaching load of six classes, consisting of some thirty pupils each. It took more stamina than I could effectively muster without straining. It was an amazing situation, a manic depressive teaching extremely active sixth graders. They really do have a lot of energy at that age. It is natural for kids to tap their pencils on their desks, for example, but it was hard on my nerves. So I was again seeing a psychiatrist. But for the life of me, I can't remember his or her name. All he or she did was prescribe pills and take up the valuable time I needed for school work.

Allen was having a problem with his job. The oil company he contracted for was folding, and he was looking for work as a consultant. This added to my pressures. Sometimes I didn't think I could finish the afternoon. First, second, and third periods usually received my best efforts despite the Thorazine aftereffects. By lunch I would be crying to Dad that I couldn't make it. He would give me some crackers and cheese and reassure me. He would try to bolster my spirits and it always worked.

At night I began to crawl into bed at earlier and earlier hours, leaving my lesson plans and students' papers for my father and Allen to grade. By the end of the year even my precocious nine-year-old daughter, Jamie, was helping grade my students' papers. Allen prepared my lesson plans and I copied them over. It was all wrong. This was not the way things had been at Aarmour. There I had been an idealistic, creative teacher who took a lot of pride in her classroom work and student achievements. I had energy and enthusiasm in my early days of teaching, in the 1970's. Maybe if I hadn't kept comparing those days with this effort ten years later it would have been easier.

Now that I look back on this experience, I did make a hard effort to keep my sense of humor in the class room. I truly liked my minority, low income stratum students and I think they realized it. I'm too though on myself sometimes. Actually the kids were pretty well behaved, but the least bit of their talking out of place disturbed my equilibrium. So I began to use too often two words that I myself hated, "Shut up!" To kids, these are probably the harshest words in the English vocabulary.

One day I said, "Shut up," followed by telling my students that if they forgot the heading on their papers I would not grade them. Every student wrote the following title: "Sit down, shut up and do your work." They had gotten my message, but I didn't feel the better for it.

The goal for me was to complete the school year so my record would be clean. I can't remember February of that year very well. I spent a "sick leave period" in a little hospital near home. In the five days I was there I received massive doses of Thorazine and a return to lockup. I don't think I was very sick, just strung out. If I remember correctly, I actually signed myself into that hospital thinking I could get a few days rest and loving care. When would I learn? Allen got me out. I can't even remember the name of the hospital.

Without taking any time to recuperate (and without anyone at the school knowing where I'd been) I went right back to the classroom. My speech was garbled from all the medications I had received, and the kids could barely understand me. Whoever said, "Life is easy?" Certainly not me.

That year was tough. But I kept hanging on. The principal came in one day to evaluate my teaching. I jumped up from behind my desk and proceeded to follow all the wonderful teaching procedures I knew, but hadn't had enough energy to use. I always did know how to put on a model lesson at the drop of a hat. If the students were amazed at me they showed no signs and responded in a most proper form. My principal loved it and gave me an evaluation of "Outstanding." But I just didn't have the strength and nerves to do it every day. And that's what I really wanted to do. I wanted to be the perfect, well-liked teacher again.

I know that I used some good concepts teaching the kids that year, even with my handicap. I imparted the wonderful advice of the ancient Greeks, concepts like the idea of moderation, the "golden mean," doing nothing to excess. If I'd followed these concepts myself as I do now, perhaps it would have been one of the happiest years I would have experienced in a long while.

The year ended. I had made it, thanks in large part to nice, cooperative students, Allen, Dad, and Jamie. She was only too happy and proud that her mother was teaching again. Together we made great memories that year, and that's what it's all about, isn't it? But despite my principal's evaluation and an offered teaching contract renewal, I put a hold on my teaching career. I didn't think my family was up to it.

Chapter 22

TOMORROW IS ANOTHER DAY

Vivien Leigh has always been one of my favorite actresses. This talented woman, who played Scarlett O'Hara in *Gone with the Wind,* was acknowledged to suffer from bipolar disorder. She never understood her condition, and in the end it overwhelmed her. She was gallant in her battle and hated some of the things she did while manic. After an episode, she would write apologies to all those people she thought she had hurt. She lost her beloved "Larry" Olivier because of her illness. He couldn't handle it. Why does that sound familiar?

But like Scarlett and me, Vivien Leigh firmly believed that, "Tomorrow is another day." There is always hope and we can live for our dreams.

Lawrence Olivier had many outstanding attributes. However, we can infer that he unfortunately lacked an ability to cope with Vivien's mania. Perhaps had this grand actor had some lessons from my Allen, his life story might have had a different final curtain.

You'll see what I mean in this conversation I wrote down before signing myself into that unremembered hospital in 1981.

CONFLICT: YOU ARE MY HEART, YOU ARE MY SOUL

It started with Allen and me in the living room of our apartment. I was writing furiously, oblivious to everything around me.

ALLEN: "Honey, you're starting to get manic. You're working yourself up and getting high. Please take your pills and come to bed."

JUDY: "No, please. My head is full of ideas and I want to write them all down. I'm going to stay up all night and write. I know I can finish this play for my students."

ALLEN: "Judy, listen to me for God's sake. You're going to make me break the promise I chose to make to you when we were married. You're going to make me put you in the hospital."

JUDY: "You're bluffing. You promised. You said you wouldn't."

ALLEN: "But you're making it impossible for me to control the spiraling you're on."

JUDY: "You're right." Her voice was vicious. "Nobody can control me. I'm free! Don't call the hospital. Why don't you just lock me in the bedroom. I don't need much space. Just let me have my tablet and my pen. I'll be just fine. And I'm not taking my Thorazine. You want to dope me up. Just try and put me in the hospital. I don't need you. I don't need any one!" She laughed that chilling manic laugh.

ALLEN: "You can stay up and write but don't ever say you love me again. You've pushed me as far as I'm going to be pushed." There was a look of frustration in his eye as he took a menacing step toward me.

JUDY: "No, God, no. My God, it's happening again like it did with my brother. Don't hit me! Don't hit me!" Allen continued his advance, apparently ready to grab my tablet. "No. Please! Don't tear up my thoughts. I'll take my pills. Only don't destroy my writing." He handed me my pills, which I swallowed quickly. I began to relax even though I was still shaken. The medication works quickly.

JUDY: "I'll never forget the look in your eyes," I said as I quieted down. "It's the same look my father had in Austin last fall when I thought he was going to hit me. I can still hear him saying that I'd never live to be thirty-five. Then he said that if I thought I was going to make a fool of him I had another think coming. But I wasn't scared of him, or you for that matter. I knew you wouldn't hurt me."

ALLEN: "Don't ever defy me like that again. It could make me lose self-control. You injured my pride when you laughed at me." He took me in his arms.

JUDY: "I understand, my darling. But please don't ever say I can't say I love you. If that ever happened, I would swallow the whole bottle of pills. Honey, I'm sorry if I hurt your pride. I wasn't laughing at you. I was laughing at something else. I don't know what."

ALLEN: "Let's lie down, now. You'll put your head on my shoulder. You'll like that."

JUDY: "Okay, honey. I'm getting tired."

We moved into the bedroom and lay down, my head on his upper arm.

ALLEN: "When you're like that it hurts too much, because I love you too much. If you can laugh at me and say you don't need me, I get angry. I only want to protect you. You are my heart, you are my soul."

Chapter 23

VOLUNTEERING FOR SERVICE

During my year at the middle school (1981-1982), I decided that I wanted to keep a pledge I had made to myself many times while I was confined in various hospitals. I wanted to make female psychiatric patients feel better about themselves and their appearance. I wanted to work with them on their make-up and hair. I made numerous phone calls and finally found a volunteer coordinator, a Mrs. Sheller, who was interested in my offered services. During a visit with her at Peace Hospital, I told her about my not so savory psychiatric record. I also told her that I was clean now and teaching in a public school. I turned on all of my persuasive charm and described the program I had in mind.

I would visit every Saturday and bring cosmetics, combs, and mirrors that I would purchase with my own funds. Using these, I intended to assist and guide the female patients in their attempts at better grooming. I told her that I firmly believed that when you looked better you felt better. Who would know this more than I? When I was a patient in now too many hospitals, nobody would let me have my lipstick. They used my requests for my lipstick as a carrot, to get me to behave.

Appropriate, quiet behavior was rewarded with the cosmetics. They didn't understand that my wearing lipstick actually promoted my appropriate behavior. I felt more civilized wearing it. It shouldn't have been used as bribery and held over me. I told the coordinator that I wanted to help patients in similar situations.

"If I accomplish nothing else," I said, "it would help to alleviate some of the terrible boredom patients experience in their wards on Saturdays." Mrs. Sheller's piercing eyes seemed to ask, "Can I trust her?" She concluded that the merits of this experiment made it worth trying.

I asked her to let me forego wearing the volunteer uniform. "I've always hated any kind of uniform," I explained. "It reminds me of prison dress and hospital gowns. Besides, I want the patients to see me as I really dress." Mrs. Sheller nodded her agreement, adding that she didn't care if I told anyone and everyone my background. I was moved by her confidence in me.

So, Saturday mornings revolved around something that I really wanted to do. I received a great reception. The patients called me the "make-up lady." At first they thought I was with Avon. Everyone would usually be in bed when I got there. I proceeded to rouse them and encourage them that they could look prettier.

I ended up teaching basic skin care and good hygiene. Then we would put a little color on their pale faces. I never had a problem with behavior. They were all very eager to work with me.

I tried bringing my excess clothes, but that was a bad idea. Too much stealing. Since it was a welfare hospital there was just too much need and desire for new things.

Many Saturdays Allen or my father came with me. In the beginning we brought donuts. We soon found out that that, too, was a bad idea. The sugar made them hyperactive.

The experiment turned out great. But I used a lot of my not-too-plentiful energy. Teaching school was still keeping me all too busy, but I managed to continue this unusual means for helping others for more than two years. It was a pleasant and rewarding part of my life that I will never forget. When the patients smiled at their "new look," I noticed that some of them stopped the shaking, singing, or chanting associated with their illnesses, which made this even more rewarding. How true the saying, "Every little bit helps," and the song title, "Little Things Mean A Lot."

I still love working with cosmetics, and I look at a clean face as an artist looks at a clean canvas. It helps me relax. When I sit at my vanity and listen to my radio, I'm content and consider myself fortunate.

I just wish a program like this could be more widespread for all hospital patients. Just consider how groaty and messy one feels sitting in bed in any hospital room, not just a psychiatric ward!

Chapter 24

GET DRESSED!

When I was a patient, the things the staff could always use for behavior modification, or in plain words to bribe me, were my lipstick and hair rollers. These were taken away from me at the outset of my stay. I would proceed to go around with a wild look. I felt very messy without my two props, and wearing a hospital gown to boot. Hospital gowns are certainly some of the least flattering garments ever designed. I believe they destroy a patient's dignity. It remains filed in the back of my mind that the Nazis took away the clothes of their prisoners and put them in striped pajamas in order to destroy their dignity and humanity.

One time when I was doing volunteer work at Peace Hospital, there were two boys of about nineteen years of age lying in their hospital beds, wearing pajamas and staring into space. One boy was hooked into an intravenous system whose tubes fed through his nose. The other would get out of his bed to wander aimlessly and barefoot around the ward from time to time.

I spoke to them both. "What do you think you're doing in your pajamas at one o'clock in the afternoon?" And to the second boy, "Where are your shoes? Do you think these floors are hygienically clean?" Then back to both, "How do you expect to get out of here if you can't get yourself dressed?"

One of the boys replied that someone had said there was something wrong with his head.

"There probably is if you let yourself be treated like an animal," I retorted.

"What should we do?" the youth questioned.

"Ask for your clothes for starters," I snapped. "And don't take no for an answer."

The more mobile youth walked to the aide in charge who was sitting in a chair, lazily tilted back against the wall and reading a paperback. "We'd like our clothes, please," the boy declared. The aide sneered at him and asked him coldly where he thought he was going that he needed his clothes.

The boy pleaded. The aide apparently didn't want to be bothered. "It's foolishness," he snapped. "Do you see anybody else around here with clothes on?"

"Yes," I broke into the conversation, "but they're all crazy. Why don't you just give him his clothes? It'll restore his dignity."

The aide eyed me suspiciously. "Who are you, anyway?"

"I'm a troublemaker who's going to raise hell unless you give these boys their clothes," I retorted.

"Well, it's against regulations," he said firmly.

Just as firmly, I said, "Put down that paperback and show me any such regulation."

He gave up trying to take the easy way out, put down his paperback, and in a matter of minutes returned with the boys' clothing. He practically threw the garments at them. I left the ward so as not to infringe on the boys' modesty as they dressed.

The more mobile youth sorted out and put on his things. Then, without prompting, he helped the one with the IV tubes dress himself.

When both were dressed, I returned to smiles all around. Both thanked me.

"I feel like a real person again," said the one without the tubes.

"Hey, lady, I think I actually feel better, too," said the other.

The aide, buried again in his paperback, ignored the significance of the entire episode.

Chapter 25

CAN A MENTAL PATIENT FIND SUCCESS AND HAPPINESS AS A POLITICIAN?

1982 was an election year in Houston, Texas. It was the year I ran for the City Council and it was the year I started getting better.

But, it's always darkest before the dawn. I was driving Allen and my father wild. I even made my father cry by yelling at him to leave and return to Philadelphia.

"Don't pick on me," he pleaded.

I was yelling and screaming a lot. Nothing could please me. I felt as if I were crawling out of my skin. Finally, Allen, now the senior scientist for a major company, couldn't take the mood swings anymore and moved out. He left behind a good-bye note signed with a picture of a broken heart.

He wrote, "I wish you all the luck in the world that is possible." Because he was one of my two anchors, I knew I would need it.

I didn't take Allen's leaving too seriously. After all, he had a three-week lecture tour of Japan, China and Tibet scheduled for that time, anyway. But my mind was affected. I started to think there was going to be a great flood in Houston (which could be entirely possible with the city's poor drainage system). I believed the "bad" people would not make it home from work. I began reading the newspaper for signs that it was about to happen. Instead, I found articles bemoaning the traffic snarl and mass transit problems. For some reason this captured my manic mind.

I would solve Houston's transportation problems. Since I've always been a problem-solving person, it was not too difficult to come up with a tentative plan. Now I needed a base of power. I would run for Mayor. Does this sound like delusions of grandeur or what? However, even I could see that this plan was crazy. So I settled for aiming at a seat on the City Council. I would be running against a five-time incumbent. I got the required petition for candidacy signed (25 names) and proudly turned it in at City Hall.

My political career came to a grinding halt when the police arrested me for parking my car across four lanes of traffic on the busiest street in Houston. After all, I had to stop the bad people from getting home. To add one extra theatrical touch, I bought some halloween masks and wore them in my locked, traffic-blocking car. This led to a short trip to the psychiatric ward, with a pit stop at the local police station. Luckily I was still on Allen's health insurance plan, or it would have been very unpleasant for me. I started out my hospital stay by kicking my doctor in the groin. Not an auspicious beginning, shall we say?

From there it was lockup, hospital gowns, and my classic singing and dancing of Hava Nagila. By this time even I was getting tired of this routine.

Three weeks passed. I began to touch base with reality, thanks to a Dr. Jane Berg. Along with the usual Thorazine she gave me a lithium level test. She was amazed at the low level of lithium in my blood. "Lithium is a salt," she explained. "In manic-depressives, when the blood's lithium level gets too low, the person gets high." She started me on lithium pills.

After nine long years of suffering and twelve commitments to mental hospitals, shock treatments and inhumane torture, it appeared that my entire problem was that I suffered a readily curable chemical imbalance. Simple, eh? Then why wasn't I given lithium earlier by the numerous physicians and psychiatrists from whom I sought help. Lithium treatment for bipolar disorders had already been known for over sixty years. Why hadn't I been treated for lithium deficiency long ago, and why wasn't the potiental for lithium correcting my manic behavior ever mentioned? Could it be that providing such a simple remedy wouldn't have been profitable for my previous doctors? Oh, well, as Stuart would say, "You win some, you lose some." He also said, "That's the way the ball bounces." Anyway, I was out of the hospital before I could say, "Jack Robinson." This episode must have been in September.

It was to be a long journey back to normalcy, but I made up my mind that an alumna of twelve mental establishments could do it. My town house looked great. I found Allen's broken heart note, which I had just dumped in a drawer, reread it, and decided that I would make it all up to him. He certainly deserved to see the other side of me. And besides, he always said I had potential.

My father was there when the phone rang. Was I still running for City Council? It was the *Houston Chronicle* wanting a personality profile. Without batting an eyelash I answered in the affirmative. "Sure," I said, "I'll send my biography." I proceeded to do so. Of course, I left out the part about having been recently released from a psychiatric hospital. Anyway, I was starting over, a clean slate. I had business cards printed and started speaking to the public in meetings that included the three other candidates running for the post. I even went on a local television show and managed to speak coherently and effectively on the campaign issues. How was I able to do this? Frankly, to this day, it's a mystery to me. Maybe a bit of residual mania remained in my brain.

I even researched and published a three-page "white paper" for solving Houston's traffic mess. I thought the paper was professional and darn good, too. Maybe I had more potential than even Allen had dreamed. I believed, even at that time, that God had plans for me. Maybe politics was that career.

Anyway, I was a lot less irritable and a lot more stable than I'd been in years. All I had to do was take lithium to even me out and Thorazine to sleep. The situation was looking brighter.

In the middle of the campaign, Allen returned from his lecture tour. My father and I met him at the airport. He was actually glad to see me. It wasn't too hard to persuade him that the bad Judy had left forever. Maybe we could lead a normal, happy life with my lithium helping me.

Allen was more supportive than ever. He helped my then seventy-seven-year-old father put up my campaign posters around the district. Am I lucky or what to have such great men in my corner?

Election day came. All the ten incumbents on the City Council were re-elected. But post-election statistics showed that more than three thousand people voted for me. More than for any candidate except the incumbent. This did a lot to restore my confidence in myself. I guess maybe I should have used the slogan: "All The Way With Judy K" rather than, "Vote For Feder, There Is None Better." I hear that Houston still has its traffic problems. Maybe they are more ready for me now.

Judy Feder is a candidate for City Council, District F

Judy Feder

Judy Feder is seeking the Houston City Council, District F position to promote her views on transportation, education, public services, and senior citizens.

Feder's fresh approach to improving things is based on her formal training and experience in "problem solving". She attended Michigan State University, majoring in Political Science, History and Education and graduated with high honors.

Feder prides herself in achieving the solution to each problem in a step-by-step manner, without creating a host of other problems. Indeed, she believes that by using sechel (good Yiddish common sense), problems can be related and solved simultaneously.

One of Feder's main projects recently has been delving into the transportation snarl. After interviewing Hector Garcia of Metro, she went to work writing up a tentative solution to avoid gridlock. It is a multi-faceted approach, taking into consideration all phases of transportation and giving a new slant to many of the old ideas.

Another of her concerns is the proposed library budget cut. "Books are very important to our youth, and I believe the Houston Public Library is excellent and should be applauded for their topnotch personnel, informational services, and film library, among many other areas of their operation."

"I need data...I've got good ideas," says Feder. "But I need a forum from which people will listen to me. As Martin Luther King said, I, too, have a dream. I dream of a world with peace and opportunity for all. Some men see things as they are and say 'why?' I dream things that never were and say 'why not?'"

Chapter 26

HAPPY DAYS ARE HERE AGAIN

Allen and I moved to Silver Spring, Maryland, a suburb of Washington, D. C. in 1988 when he accepted a position with a major aerospace company. I loved it in Silver Spring. It was almost like going back to my roots. It was only 165 miles from Philadelphia, and our apartment was located in the same complex as that of my cousin, Frank Watzman.

I think Frankie deserves a word here because he's really a great, generous, funny guy who is very important to me. I've sort of adopted him. He is more to me than a third cousin. He is my friend. Frankie looked out for me during my stay in Maryland. When Allen traveled, which was often, it would be either hamburgers or banana pancakes a la Frank at his place. We'd laugh and talk. Slowly, the whole story unfolded. He believes I am special and I do feel special when I'm in his company.

I think Frankie is in his eighties, but he acts so young that his actual age is a mystery which he carefully protects. Anyway, he was good company in Silver Spring. And now that we've moved on, I just pick up the phone whenever I'm lonesome for him.

Shortly after moving to Silver Spring I took a job as a receptionist. I kept it for only seven months because I found the work so boring. Also, my insignificant salary was eaten up by the area's high cost of living. On the plus side, however, that job did get me out of the apartment.

After I quit as a receptionist, Allen again took things into his own hands and started answering want ads on my behalf. One was for a teacher of secular subjects in a nearby Hebrew private school. The teaching was in the afternoons and the students were fourth graders. I interviewed well with the Rabbi principal, a delightful, intelligent personality. I immediate liked him. He loved kids, and showed a terrific sense of humor. The way he talked about the students in the school during the interview, and the photo album that he proudly showed me of student activities led me to believe he was a good and fair man. I later found out this was a correct appraisal.

The school was only four miles from our apartment. This was really the new beginning I'd been waiting for, a real second chance. From the first day of school I was comfortable and confident. The healing process of the last eight years had closed many of my old wounds. I again began using the teaching methods I hadn't used in years, and I achieved excellent results in doing so.

I encountered only one significant problem. In my students' enthusiasm, the noise level the class generated was becoming too high for both effective learning and comfort. It was getting difficult to maintain control. I didn't want to curb my students' desire to participate. Yet, I wanted to instill the courtesy and formality of raised hands in response to questions I asked and to gain my attention. There had to be good discipline in order for us to accomplish all I had in mind.

And then I found a piece of paper with a smiling face decal on it. Why not hand out one of these when I discovered a good youngster having a good day. The discovery came in the nick of time.

My plan was simple. I would give a deserving student a Smile-O-Gram for excellent behavior. Each Smile-O-Gram bore my signature to make it official. Pupils who received the most Smile-O-Grams at the end of the semester would receive little prizes.

My students just loved the whole thing, and so did their parents. The kids took their Smile-O-Grams home and stuck them on their refrigerators. Suddenly the kids were raising their hands and waiting patiently to be called upon. They were walking quietly in straight lines to Phys. Ed. and other activities. They were practicing special courtesy and thoughtfulness.

In short, this formerly boisterous class of seventeen became a joy. From then on it was a piece of cake. The principal loved it. "I don't know whether you make the kids look good," he told me, "or they make you look good." I appreciated the praise.

I was at that school for only four months before Allen told me his company was transferring him to Huntsville, Alabama, but they were very happy months for me. I remember thinking at the time Allen broke the news to me that maybe it was for the best. Now nothing could spoil my memories of those four months. I hadn't overdone it, and my sense of humor in and out of the classroom was excellent.

So was the student humor as expressed by one little girl the day I came to class with a cold. "I'm really not feeling well today," I confided. I've got this bad cold, and I'd appreciate your extra cooperation."

Melanie raised her hand and with a deadpan expression said, "Don't tell me your troubles and I won't tell you mine," which is probably the most down-to-earth advice I have ever received. No one wants to hear you pour out your troubles and complaints. There's enough of that in this world.

I've tried to tell an upbeat story in this book. I'm not complaining about life. I'm not asking for sympathy. Life, in general, is taking what comes, getting up and coming back for more. It is about hope for the future. I think everything in our lives happens for a reason. Sometimes we don't understand what it is, but as long as we hang in there and keep our faith in God we'll be all right. Consider that this philosophy comes from making more than 20 stops in mental hospitals.

I was really quite surprised when I had to tell my students that I was leaving. There were tears shed all around the classroom. I think I shed a few, too. In my last day as their teacher, we had a great party, and the four Smile-O-Gram winners proudly received their awards. Everyone won something. Many gave me Smile-O-Grams. The one I liked best said, "Mrs. Feder had a great four months."

Thus ended a truly wonderful chapter in my life. One of my favorite mementos came from a teacher's aide. It makes wonderful reading when obstacles arise in the road of life.

Dear Judy,

Just a note to let you know I am really sorry you have to leave. I will miss doing science with you and getting excited about Maryland history.

I haven't known you very long, but in the short time we interacted I learned that you are very interested in people and reaching out to them. I noticed that you always got people to talk about themselves, a sure sign of a concerned and considerate person as well as a good listener.

As for me, you really made me feel appreciated and I appreciate that!

When you told us you were leaving, your words sounded sad; not just your words, but your whole body seemed sad. I really felt for you.

I don't know how you feel or believe about God, but I'd like to share something with you, take it or leave it.

I have moved around a lot and have gradually learned that God goes with me everywhere I go and has fascinating plans for me there. When He closes a door in one place He opens another somewhere else and His plans are always far more fantastic than anything I could have imagined. Case in point: Evangelical Christian Fanatic (me) working in an Orthodox Jewish school! I think God has something really great waiting for you. Move down there expecting to find out what it is.

I will miss you.

Love,
S/Charlene

P.S. When you find out what the fantastic thing is, drop me a line.

Chapter 27

BLEEDING TO DEATH

I've already told you Allen's version of how we met. But mine is simpler—I was bleeding to death in a gutter in Austin. Allen saw me, picked me up, bandaged me and saved me.

There may or may not be total truth in this story, but it kind of indicates the shape I was in back then. I felt unloved, ugly, and sick. Allen made me feel beautiful. He still does. He sees more of my good points than I do. Allen is a creature of habits. Some good, some not so good. I have been working with him to tone down the bad habits and accentuate the many good ones. After all, I'm a teacher, aren't I?

Allen is an avid, pipe-smoking romantic, but also a workaholic. Along with his trait of calmness, he is sensitive and can and does get hurt easily—a barrier I try to avoid.

We have a great time together. We both like good food (there's a bond)! Allen likes for me to enjoy myself and lets me be me. I think he really enjoys my many personalities, from the "baby doll" to the "world crusader."

Until Allen developed spinal stenosis that precludes his travelling, we had great vacations together. Allen loved to travel and was a great planner and organizer. We took two cruises, did the Fountainbleu in Florida three times, explored California's Muir Woods, and enjoyed Disney World with Jamie.

Allen has made my life fun. Just sitting in our patio and talking and joking is great.

He notices my hair and my clothes and is very attentive and appreciative.

He has come through for me for every one of the hospitalizations I have had since we first met. For these austere events he invariably first contacted the psychiatrist and social or case worker and put pressure on them to treat me as a person rather than a mental case number. He would go through all my things at home to bring exactly what I wanted and needed in the hospital. He visited with me in the hospital at every opportunity, although it initially took overcoming the mental block he has against hospitals. And when he would visit, he would bring me any type of take-out dinner I craved to supplement or replace hospital fare.

He also was *always* polite and friendly to my fellow patients, even when they aggressively hit on us for food and money. He seemed to sense the right thing to do, the right thing to say, every time. He knew I'd have to stay with these people after he returned home.

When we celebrated our seventeenth wedding anniversary (Allen told people that it was seventeen years without time off for good behavior), I decided it was safe to say Allen was committed to be my helper and morale builder for the duration of our lives together. He always said he "saw my potential."

I have great abilities to motivate people. I guess it comes from my years as a teacher. Anyway, I like to think I motivate Allen, partly by love, partly by companionship, and partly by positive reinforcement, to be the best he can be in helping me reach my potential. His best suits me fine. I can even live with the constant pipe smoke, and believe that my allergic reactions to it have cleared up. Now I just find it unpleasant. Allen Feder without a pipe, chocolate, coffee, or ice cream? It'll never happen. But he's a good man, and I love that good in him.

One day, Allen and I were sitting in our living room watching a Nelson Eddy, Jeanette McDonald movie, "Rose Marie." It was a great oldie and we were really enjoying it. Then Nelson Eddy sang beautifully to Jeanette McDonald, "Rose Marie, I love you, I'm always thinking of you." When the movie ended, Allen started singing out to me, "Judy Arlene, I love you, I'm always thinking of you."

After that, every day at 1:00 p.m. when he phoned me from his office—this was before he retired—he sang it to me. Even without the song, there is no doubt in my mind that Allen loves me. His love has surely been tested. He stayed with me through the BAD YEARS. And he put up with quite a lot. Whenever I would get high, I would point out his every fault, real and imaginary. I remember even calling him a "shithead" once. He really didn't like that one.

Now, I usually call him "Honey" and mean it. I just want to be the good Judy and make him happy. When I get irritable and snap at Allen, he responds with gentleness. He'll sit down and put his arm around me and we'll talk. Or we'll lie down and he'll extend his arm for me to nestle in. He calls it "cricking" and claims a crick is the answer to the world's problems. Maybe he's right.

Every night when he arrived home from work he'd find me and give me a kiss, no matter how tired he was. He trusts me with his life. At least that's what he always tells me. He finds all the best qualities in me and fosters them. He listens to me. Really listens. He usually understands what I am trying to say. Even when I don't.

He says he saw my potential years ago. Probably many years before I could even believe that I had any potential.

We sleep in separate bedrooms because I wake up so much during the night and he is a light sleeper. But his spirit is right there next to me. When he used to go away on business trips I couldn't sleep at all. But those days are over. I know God takes care of me *all* the time.

Allen is definitely a romantic. He wrote me beautiful poetry until I discouraged him permanently during one of my irritable periods.

Allen appointed me his social director. It's a non-paying job with a low budget, but it's definitely a great honor.

Allen is so special to me. He is my rock and since he is a geologist by profession, this is an apt description. "Allen Martin, I love you!"

Chapter 28

JAMIE

Since I've already told you about Sam and Allen, I guess this is as good a time as any to present some more things about my daughter, Jamie, who continues as an important part of my life. When she was 24 and a senior in the University of Houston's School of Law, she asked me who was the hero of my book. Shamelessly I replied, "I am, of course. It's my book—why shouldn't I be?" I told her that she could write a book about her life. Then she could be the heroine.

Actually, Jamie is very heroic. She lived through several of my manic attacks, was propagandized against me by her father, succeeded in getting herself into shape following a long, hard struggle with excess weight, and fought for her academic life through a ridiculous course called Organic Chemistry. She inherited my genes. She is a survivor. I have stopped worrying about Jamie. Allen and I agree that she will make it to the finish line and be something wonderful. But I believe Allen will always hold her in his heart as "Li'l Jim," the precocious eight-year-old to whom he became so attached.

She loves kids and would love to be a child psychologist. She would be a great one. However, monetary considerations, the lack of available jobs, and mostly her father, on whom she is dependent, forced her to change from psychology to law.

Jamie is a dreamer. She dreams big—big vacations for us, owning a big, beautiful car, wearing designer clothes. It used to be that she couldn't compromise with her dreams, but I now believe she is getting more malleable.

She's fun to be with, and I think I've created a clone. She has a little of my offbeat sense of humor. I've tried to impress her with the value of humor. It can save you at some of the most traumatic points in your existence.

The only thing or person we basically differ about is her father. Stuart is still really important to her; by now the reader has captured my opinion of him. For many years I condoned her image of him, but now I'm calling a spade a spade. She's had both Stuart and me as role models. We are as different as night and day. She had a chance to learn from both of us. Only time will tell which of our influences will be the most impressive or important.

If I am to believe her letters, birthday, Mother's Day cards, Valentine cards and her messages on these, Jamie loves me very much and is quite proud of me. Of course, I'm a sucker for the praise and lap it up.

Jamie is my friend as well as my daughter. We laugh a lot when we're together. She's spent a couple of summers and vacation trips with Allen and me, and they were wonderful. I even got to play the Mom that I hadn't been years ago, and more.

She knows a lot now and it's more difficult for me to use positive reinforcement and such on her. She sees right through it.

Jamie is extremely pretty—with makeup, she's a knockout. Stubbornly she refuses to wear cosmetics. She has big brown eyes and long brown hair. I think she feels lucky not to be a redhead like her mother. She doesn't think she is pretty. I've tried to bolster her confidence, but she's hard to convince.

I really believe that the early years of her life and my ill-ness strengthened her. I really miss her when she's not with me. We've taken trips, just the two of us. We vacationed in San Francisco and Atlanta. She's a great traveler. Better than I. I miss her while just writing about her.

I was once in a playful mood and said to her, "Just blow me down and call me Scrappy." Later she sent me a card. At the bottom of it she wrote that I should wave the card and say, "Scrappy." Of course it made me laugh.

She once told me she's not sure there is a God. The hard parts of her life must have made her doubt. I hope she can see someday, as I do, the greatness of God and His wonder and His love. Then she will find the happiness that she is obviously lacking.

I am Baby Doll 1 to Allen. She is Baby Doll 2. I always tell people that I am just too young to have a 24 year-old daughter. Actually, I feel younger when I am around her.

Even when she was eight years old she was gentle and supportive. When I'd get somewhat high and edgy, she'd come over and sit next to me and stroke my arm. When she stopped asking me, "Are you all right?" I knew I was better.

What would my world be without Jamie? I just don't want to find out. Perhaps, as you read the following with her expressions of feelings for me, you will understand why:

Dear Mom:

It seems as if we've always been close...and as I get older, I find myself treasuring that closeness more and more. It's nice having someone who really knows and understands me, someone with whom I can always be myself. You may not know it, but your support and faith in me have pulled me through more times than I can count....

I don't know what I'd do without you in my life.

You're a wonderful mother and a very special friend to me.

HAPPY MOTHER'S DAY.

You make my life special by just being there.
Love always,
Jamie
1990

Dear Mom,

I want to thank you for being my sounding board these past few weeks and for helping me keep my sanity. There is no one else I could have or would have been able to unload all that on and I'm glad you stood by me. It's just that I want to be with you so much.

Love,
Jamie
1991

Chapter 29

MY FAVORITE PSYCHIATRIST

In 1990, when Allen and I moved to Huntsville, I found Maximilian Grant, who improved my mental state quite effectively. He was affectionately known to his friends and clients as Max. He did not pretend to practice psychiatry or any other medicine, but his methods, personality, and attitude helped me to avoid the conventional psychiatric establishment and still provided the advantage of all the good things professional psychiatry is supposed to offer. In short, Max, like Allen, made me feel good about myself.

His office was not a quiet, private, book-lined, leather-couched room. It was a rather noisy, mirrored, sink-lined parlor with tilting chrome chairs and unction bottles everywhere. It was a beauty salon in one of Huntsville's busiest department stores. Max was my hair stylist.

When I arrived for my weekly visit I left all the cares of the world behind, prepared to be pampered and enjoyed myself. Max was a great listener and definitely non-judgmental. He actually encouraged me to ventilate more than any psychiatrist had up to that time. He cracked jokes, confided "secrets" and above all encouraged me to be myself and relax.

But the amazing thing was that, while everyone in the salon—clients and practitioners alike—were enjoying themselves and having a good time, Max kept working to create a beautiful hairdo for me. And he did it in three quarters of an hour!

Max often complained that I wore my hair in the same style for so long he could do it in his sleep. Max had more spunk than to merely accept "the customer is always right" philosophy. He spoke up, when necessary, and won his customers' greatest respect. But he knew that in my case, as with other things, I preferred the status quo, so he humored me. Consequently, between the two of us, I wasn't surprised when perfect strangers stopped me and complimented me on my hairdo.

Then and now I firmly believe that when a person looks nice and feels pretty, she also feels good about her entire self. I think the psychiatric profession is missing this important point. I have gotten more confidence per dollar spent at the hair salon than I ever did in any psychiatrist's leather-couched office.

Everyone on the Huntsville salon's staff was friendly, warm, and caring. Maybe that's due to Brandy Gross, the manager. She had a knack for bringing out the best in people. She called 'em like she saw 'em, and once attributed all of my problems to bad dentistry. That remark came directly after I pulled out my ill-fitting bridgework and tossed it in her waste basket in disgust.

The clients and staff of that salon were like a family. They worried about each other. When I wasn't sleeping well, and prepared for a trip to Philadelphia, Marvin, another hair stylist, came over with a warning. "When you change planes in Memphis, don't go to the Elvis Presley Museum. You might fall asleep and they'd make a bust of your head and put it next to Elvis's." Thanks for the warning, Marvin.

Chapter 30

FROM THE DIARY OF A MANIC: REGRESSION

March 2, 1993

I awoke at 6:30 in the morning today. It rained the entire day and I stayed inside. I think I've got things under control. I'm treating all the symptoms properly and there's nothing to worry about, yet. I took 50 mg more of Thorazine last night and slept for nine hours. Without it I shudder to think where I'd be. I've increased my Lithobid pill consumption from five to six. I can't understand why this is happening with all the lithium I take. And I *know* I haven't missed taking it. I'm really careful.

Okay, let me check off the danger spots. I'm not hungry. But I don't want to lose any more weight. I'm being extra careful about my eating. I ate a lot of nourishing and high fiber food today. It keeps up my strength and gets rid of my poisons.

I didn't make one phone call today. That's always a dead giveaway, my constant need to use the phone.

My sense of humor is gone. Nothing can help that. What's there to laugh at? This is the big time. This is serious.

Maybe when I get my hair done on Thursday I'll laugh with the beauty parlor gang. But not too much. I must remember that. So far I've hidden it well. Allen hasn't the least suspicion. I haven't picked on him or talked his head off and I'm trying to keep my more controversial opinions to myself.

Allen should have noticed the mania my mind is experiencing by now, shouldn't he? (Maybe it's because it's been ten years since my last attack.) I'm a great actress, that's true. and I intend to play this one out.

I want to use the creativity and imagination I feel to do some good. Maybe I can solve a few world problems that need solving. Is there anything wrong with this?

I just counted them. I've got 290 lithobid tablets left. That's lucky. That's about a two months supply, taking six a day. I'll have to go and see my doctor in about a month. That means a lithium level test. That's what's strange. How can it possibly be low? I haven't missed my lithium. I think I said that, didn't I?

I even wrote to Daddy today. That was hard to do. I wanted to mention my articles and this book. That's too much for him right now.

Last night I barely managed to sit still long enough to watch the movie Allen put on the VCR. I wanted to be in motion. To be doing or accomplishing something. Luckily it was an interesting and well-acted movie and I ended up enjoying it. I listened to the radio all day and heard God's message through the particular songs that were played. I feel close to God through nature and music.

March 3, 1993

I had a scary dream last night. I dreamed that I went back with Stuart. Jamie was four years old. All I wanted to do in this dream was to get back at Allen. The dream woke me at 6:00 a.m. I feel good, though, because I got ten hours sleep; just have to get enough sleep by going to bed early. I've got enough Lithobid and Thorazine to last two months. I don't really trust my doctor enough to be able to confide my plans to him. Ate my fiber, a heaping bowl, had three bowel movements and my black jeans are way too big for me!!!

I went to the mall this morning. I was tempted by several things but they're not going to get me on a buying spree. I still have lots of energy, but it seems to be well directed.

I was doing pretty well, but I slipped for the first time. I called Jamie in London, England, and talked 40 minutes to her.

I'm losing my sense of humor. I don't seem to see the funny side like I'm accustomed to doing. I want to go in many directions but am still directing my energy.

March 5, 1993

Everything is going very smoothly. I even managed to sleep till 6:30 a.m. I still think that God has plans for me and that He's shaping events to give me direction. Today I took my manuscript to a small office service. They're going to edit it and type it. The people there are really nice and it seems like I'm getting a little closer to the finish line.

Things have escalated a little bit. I've lost my appetite. I can't think of food. But I'm making myself eat my high fiber diet.

Things are progressing so well that I am more convinced than ever that my "Friend" is taking a hand. And Allen is helping me more than ever. Thank you, God.

And thank You for making the Thorazine work. Allen is not the least bit suspicious.

March 6, 1993—Saturday, 7:36 a.m.

It's sunny today. Hurrah! I've been up since 3:30 a.m. and have gotten a lot accomplished. The article on education is ready. Allen doesn't even know I've been up since 3:30. But I'd really like to get up later tomorrow. I was tired today. This is happening to slow me down, I guess.

March 8, 1993—Monday

I got up at 2:00 a.m. Went back to sleep for an hour at 4:15.

Followed usual routine. I feel fine. Very slow and logical though.

March 9, 1993—Tuesday

It's 6:30 p.m. and I'm really tired. Please, God, let me get a nice sleep tonight. I feel driven to get everything done. I know I'm manic but I'm managing to control it and still write.

I am disguising most of my symptoms. The one that's the toughest is not getting enough sleep. This could lead to trouble.

I've been extra nice to Allen today.

March 10, 1993

Got up at 2:00 a.m. and stayed up. Sleep means just a bunch of bad dreams. If I can stand the loss of sleep I think I can pull this off and utilize the mania and advanced thought processes to advantage.

March 13, 1993

Funny things are happening here.

1. The wheat muffins have vanished.

2. Blizzard over the eastern half of U.S. Blizzard in Alabama.

3. My favorite cookbook is missing.

4. There wasn't any wide ruled paper in the supermarket for my work.

All these things are probably my "Friend's" work. I can only guess His reasons. If you hadn't noticed, I'm becoming quite spiritual.

Am sleeping very little and since the Thorazine doesn't seem to be working anymore I may quit it. Anyway, 20 years of it is enough, isn't it? Lord only knows how it's been poisoning my body.

March 14, 1993

I now know God's plan for me. It's to strive to be the

best I can be and use my mania to good advantage and to keep my eyes and ears open.

March 14, 1993

It seems like I don't need much sleep and that's good because I'm not getting much at all. It was a smooth day. Allen is reassured. The voices aren't occurring as often. Like He trusts me to do the right thing. I feel in control.

Chapter 31

THORAZINE WITHDRAWAL
SPRING, 1993

After ten years of relative normalcy I began to again get "high." I couldn't or wouldn't associate this with the events of the past few weeks I had just been entering in my diary. It was immaterial to me, as I found I was now able to express my thoughts in writing. I believed that, through my writing, I would be able to accomplish the mission God had assigned me many years before. I didn't fully know what that mission was or was to be, but I firmly believed I had to get people to listen to me.

I finished an article on high fiber diets and one on improving the educational system in the United States. I was really on a roll. I found a word processing service and had it all typed. It looked very professional. I sent the fiber/weight loss article to six magazines and the education article to President Clinton, Vice President Gore, Tipper Gore, Hillery Rodham Clinton, and Alabama U. S. Senators, and Albert Teague, then the Superintendent of the Alabama State Department of Education.

I was still idealistic enough to think someone would read and evaluate my ideas. To my disappointment, all of the magazines sent polite rejections. President Clinton sent an "official postcard" saying his administration was working on education. The postcard did not refer to a single one of my ideas. How could it have when it was one of the White House's many types of form responses? Hillery Rodham Clinton sent me a supercilious letter, double talk explaining her program for education. If she gets it off the ground, I thought, it will be a miracle. And what qualifications does she have in the field of education, anyway?

Superintendent Teague sent me a wonderful letter saying he really was impressed with my suggestions and was already implementing many of them in Alabama. One out of six ain't bad.

The funny thing about this manic episode was that I hadn't missed taking my lithium until I was spiralling. Upon first feeling manic, I increased the dose to six tablets. I had been getting my lithium (Lithobid) and Thorazine from internists over the past 11 years. At that time I was keeping as far away from psychiatrists as possible.

My usual dose of Thorazine (200 mg) wasn't getting me to sleep. I had been sleeping only three to four hours a night. Not a good sign. However, I would pretend to sleep so Allen wouldn't worry. Then I would get up and listen to my "elevator" music and write a couple of chapters of this book.

Then disaster struck. I had a manic brilliant idea that I didn't need any medicine but the lithium. I proceeded to quit the Thorazine cold turkey. That was a big mistake. The essential thing needed by a person susceptible to mania is adequate sleep. While Thorazine gave me incessant nightmares, it did make me sleep, even if only for a few hours. Stopping my Thorazine had catastrophic results.

First, what I thought was Thorazine withdrawal occurred. I became nauseated all the time with stomach spasms. It got so intolerable that I couldn't even sleep at night. At first, I gritted my teeth and said, "This, too, shall pass." But it didn't.

It got worse. It was a total test of my self-control to keep from screaming out in agony. But I did have absolute control in spite of my manic tendencies. Actually, by this time I had begun to believe that if I got rid of the bad qualities associated with mania I might even be able to use its creative, problem-solving, innovative thought qualities to accomplish something good. After all, wasn't Abraham Lincoln believed to be a manic-depressive, and look what he did.

The main problem I faced was constant nausea. Finally, after three months of just Lithobid, I broke down and made an appointment with, what was at the time one of my three most dis-liked classes of professionals (lawyers headed the list, psychiatrists were second and specializing doctors were third).

So I started a search for a dedicated, knowledgeable, caring doctor. I started with the phone book, asked friends for references, settled for Allen's internist, Dr. Aubrey. My husband said she was great. For him, maybe. For me, no! She tested me, said I was in good health, although I might be having gall bladder problems, suggested that I might see a gastroenterologist. To be on the safe side, she handed me three prescriptions, one for insomnia and two for stomach upset.

In agony I rushed to Wal-Mart to have them filled and almost threw up while waiting to get these panaceas for my ail-ment. I hurried home, popped the stomach pill and waited. Instead of easing my nausea, it made it worse, although it did knock me out for the whole afternoon.

By the time Allen got home, I was sluggish and in pain. I cried. He reassured me by saying that even though the stomach pills didn't work, the sleeping pills would be great. I swallowed one with a glass of iced tea, afraid of what might happen if I didn't try.

What followed was a night of horror. I spent the waking hours vomiting, retching and gagging. I never realized how bad bad could be.

The next morning I turned to my second most disliked pro-fessionals—the psychiatrists. I hoped to find one who understood

Thorazine withdrawal and had an opening before I passed out. Allen would take off a couple of hours off from work and we'd hunt up a psychiatrist. The one we found gave me more prescriptions. My pocketbook was lighter, but the wanted miracle did not occur.

I turned to the gastroenterologist as Allen's internist had suggested. The surgeon let me convince him that everything would turn out all right if I could just get rid of a diseased gall bladder. The only problem at that time was that the gall bladder was perfectly fine. I did receive a souvenir color VCR tape of the operation and a chance to wear those beautiful hospital gowns again. But the constant nausea, gas and belching went on. It was a case of pills, pain and a constant attempt to avoid irritability and mania.

After six months, not even I could pin my problem on Thorazine withdrawal. But I clung stubbornly to my original theory. I really didn't enjoy one thing I ate during those six months, but I made myself eat. And I continued to walk two miles a day. And I drank gallons of water. Nothing helped. I couldn't figure it out. My bowel movements were regular and normal. At least I stopped vomiting and didn't lose weight. My X-rays were fine. What was this mysterious illness? Was it possible that the pill mixture would eventually cause a blowup?

In June, Allen persuaded me to join him on a business trip to Washington, D. C. I was sick, but Allen assured me that a change of scenery and a side trip to my family and friends in Philadelphia would do wonders for my morale and my health. Actually, making the trip was critical for his work and he didn't want to leave me alone in Huntsville.

We climbed into a cab at 6:30 a.m. and almost missed our flight because of dense fog. Even safely aboard the plane, we were squashed into tourist class and the take-off was delayed for two hours until the fog lifted. I thought I was going to faint in the aisle. Then, a sweet stewardess noted my near death-like appearance and moved both Allen and me to first class. I guess the thought was that with fewer people in first class, a corpse wouldn't be so noticeable. But in a way it helped, because I missed having to make a hospital run at the stopover in Nashville.

Washington was horrible. I felt lousy, and Allen spent most of his time attending business meetings. One night, to prove I wasn't manic (manic people tend to get dressed up and roam), I stayed in the hotel room the entire evening and ate only a container of cole slaw. I was determined not to show any of the manic symptoms, or at least to nip them in the bud. It was a lonely and painful experience. The past-midnight hours were torturous. Trying to keep quiet, trying not to awaken Allen, trying to sleep, and basically trying to survive.

The stay in Washington ended for me in disaster with an attack of what I prefer to call chemical poisoning or chemical interaction. Everything kicked in at the same time. Months of bad pills and experimentation with prescriptions—all pushed on me. But I took them. I paid dearly! Everything looked black. Allen suggested that I try Alka Seltzer. "Just one good burp and you'll be fine!" he said. Out of desperation, I agreed to try. That good burp never came.It was a seven-stop and fourteen-Alka Seltzer drive to Philadelphia.

The City of Brotherly Love! The city of my birth. Not necessarily famous for that fact. We stayed at the Sheraton Motel and drove back and forth to Dad's. He had become mother's nursemaid. Mom had suffered a stroke a year and a half earlier and couldn't walk. Dad took a few minutes off each day to grow his beloved raspberries and shop for food for Mom.

The five days in northeast Philadelphia were nerve shattering. I couldn't finish a meal. I had to get the mania or body strength going in order to fight the increasingly serious stomach spasms.

The world for me at this point was divided into good and bad people. My father even became bad, as I recalled with Allen the outpatient shock treatment episode he had permitted psychiatrists to give me 13 years before. He had now given me up to devote himself solely to Mom, and in my condition I resented this. Well, there was still Allen's loyalty trying to fix things for me. He wanted to take me to the University of Pennsylvania Medical Center for tests. No he wouldn't. Not if I had a breath left in my body.

My stomach was a mess, so we decided to cut our trip short and skip my visit to the local hospital. I managed to convince Allen that I was getting better and that it was unnecessary. And to this day I think that that was a smart decision, even though possibly for the wrong reason. In my condition I would have been checked in for gastric tests, but sent directly to psychiatric. Allen would have had to leave to get back to his work in Huntsville. Dad would have been forced to split his time between Mom and me. That's the way I visualized the scenario. I didn't want Daddy peeling oranges for me again. I do not do well in hospitals. That's the bottom line.

Northeast Philadelphia appeared extremely strange during our visit. The people all looked mean, dressed oddly and had weird hairdos. Everything in the great Northeast had deteriorated badly. Allen and I would double over laughing just watching many of the inhabitants of this section of Philly.

It was in Philadelphia and in D. C. that I manically envisioned the United States in a mess. I sensed that God meant for me to take an active role in trying to straighten things out. After all, hadn't I been a world's problems teacher? What better credentials than mine? I had a manic mind, a problem-solving brain, was flexible, was a history and political science teacher. Sure, I hadn't really used my brain in many years, but my thought processes were sharpening every day and my problem solving skills along with them. My biggest problem was Allen. In order for any of my future plans to work, Allen had to trust in God and believe in me. These were two big requests. I felt that this trip had been kind of pre-ordained as God's test of me and a bigger test of Allen.(The poor guy is a devout believer in God. He prays twice every day.

He had no problem trusting God. As for me and my calling....)

I had been hearing God's messages to me for 25 years, especially when my lithium level was good (I didn't know then that the lithium wasn't working for me). Sometimes I heard Him during my radio station music broadcasts. Sometimes I'd feel Him in my heart when I saw a thing of His creation that was extremely beautiful. At other times, He would come to me in my dreams. I knew I was manic—so what? But I had to convince Allen that his Baby Doll had a calling. We had many discussions, and finally, after a long walk, I believed he agreed with me (or humored me might be more appropriate?), that the world needed a lesson; that God would not allow this planet earth to continue with its evil ways. We packed our things, drove to the airport, and I barely made it to my seat on the plane. The nausea and tiredness were overwhelming.

As we finally climbed the steps to our apartment, I thanked God that I hade made it back to Huntsville. Then I wondered what would happen next....

Chapter 32

LOCKED UP AGAIN

November, 1993

After our trip to Philadelphia, Huntsville was looking better each moment. But the apartment was a *mess* and with my mania I can't stand even a little messiness. It affected my mood and made me jumpy.

I started to clear and clean things up and sent Allen down to Winn-Dixie to restock our groceries. I still hadn't recuperated from the plane flight or the horrible nausea. I hadn't had a decent amount of sleep in weeks.

When Allen got back from the supermarket I was quite nervous. I needed someone, perhaps a maid, to help in my cleaning and organization. I had never had a maid but could have used one on that particular night. Likely, this would have helped avoid the ensuing scene, which led to my fourteenth incarceration.

Allen received a phone call from a good friend in Dallas. He proceeded to laugh and talk with him for about ten minutes. While he was talking on the kitchen phone, something inside me *snapped*, an unusual phase of my mania. I found myself for the second time in 12 years raising my voice to Allen. "Can't you help me unload the dishwasher," I exploded. I knew right away by the angry frown on his face that I had made a major mistake. I forgot that he had been holding down my mania for weeks and that he was also fatigued by the trip. The phone call and levity with his friend was helping him relax. He hung up the phone and roared at me, "How dare you embarrass me in front of my friends? I won't tolerate that!"

The sound and fury of his words pulled a violent reaction from me that had been bottled up for years. I answered with cruel and nearly hysterical words. It felt great. At that point, I was not thinking of the consequences. It was just a release for me from all the pain and sleeplessness.

Allen grabbed the phone and dialed 911. I grabbed my purse and car keys and was in my car driving along University Drive, Huntsville's main drag, before Allen's 911 call could provide the assistance he needed. I didn't feel like myself. My only aim was to find somewhere safe, away from Allen, the police, doctors, hospitals and ambulances. This scene had been played before. I knew from experience with Stuart how it would end but I was going to give it a good try, so help me.

I was bone tired. I pulled into a shabby motel, paid for the room with the little cash I had and collapsed on the bed. I was wearing my now rumpled traveling outfit. I carefully took it off and folded it as neatly as I could. The clock on the radio alarm showed 10:00. I lay down in exhaustion. The next time I looked at the clock it said 12:30 a.m. So evidently I had had a little sleep without pills. I phoned Allen, who sounded very strange. He asked where I was. Something told me to hang up, so I did, without really communicating with him. If I had been in better shape I would have worked with him, but at that moment all I wanted was to be on my own and determine if I could make it. No one was going to threaten me again. I just wasn't going to accept it!

I was repulsed by the shabby, dirty, musty motel room. And I was hungry. The nausea and stomach pains reminded me that I hadn't eaten since leaving Philly. Allen always maintained that eating good food made you feel better. Even though my stomach was still upset, I had to get something into it. There was even the possibility, I thought, that food would make me feel better. So I dressed, got back in the car and headed toward the main drag again, finally pulling into a waffle and pancake restaurant. It was definitely no place for a manic person. At that early morning hour all the weirdos in town were wandering in and out of this quaint little establishment. It didn't take me long to realize I could be in danger, So I avoided the beckoning strangers and beat a hasty retreat to my car. Once in its safety, I figured an all-night supermarket would provide a safer and better source of nourishment. I went to the Winn-Dixie where I regularly shopped, and browsed for an hour and a half. It felt so good. What a nice, clean place. What a nice staff they had. Taking my few purchases and remembering my credit card, I decided I deserved a cheerful motel room and a hot bath. I knew just such a place.

Allen and I had enjoyed our stay in a beautiful apartment motel suite when we first moved to Huntsville. (I was beginning to miss Allen and some semblance of the good life we had been having together). I was right about the motel. When I got to my suite, I took a hot bath, explored the rooms, used the jacuzzi, and fell asleep for three more hours. When I awoke about 6:00 a.m. I felt well rested.

But when I put on my travel-worn clothes, they felt crumby, and my cosmetics were limited. I thought of Allen, figured he'd be getting ready for work. I really thought he'd be going to work. I thought that nothing could interfere with his going to the office.

I needed a plan. I had about $60.00 in cash. I would go to the bank when it opened at 8:30 a.m. and get the share of our savings that was rightfully mine. Then I would go to the beauty salon and get the works. I also planned on purchasing some new clothes and cosmetics. Hadn't I been going through hell?

Didn't I deserve to buy some pretty things? This was truly manic thinking. I had a closet, two bureaus and a vanity table of pretty things Allen and I had bought together and much that he had bought for me.

In the meantime, I headed to the nearest Wal-Mart and bought some essentials and a non-manic necessity, a denture cup. I truly thought I could stay at the apartment motel until I could think things out. After all, it sure was a nice place.

At 8:30 the bank doors opened. I told the clerk, who knew me, that Allen and I were moving to Atlanta and that Allen told me to withdraw all of our cash for moving expenses. I closed three accounts and left the bank with a $13,000 cashier's check and over $4,000 in cash. I really didn't have any plans for the money. It just meant safety and security to me. I learned later that the bank clerk had not bought my story. She conferred with the manager who felt obligated to call Allen, who had *not* gone to work. Allen knew me too well—knew that I would head for the hair dresser as soon as I left the bank.

That's just what I did. But I first stopped in at my local dentist to see if anything could be done to replace the ill-fitting temporary partial I was using till my dentures were ready. The receptionist said the two dentists on duty had no openings the entire day. That made me angry. I was later told that I had been abusive to the dental assistants and threw my temporary partial at them, but I remember none of that. They, too, phoned Allen to let him know of my condition.

Marquette Mall in Huntsville is a friendly, homey place and I felt safe. What could happen to me here? I went to check in for a manicure before my hair styling appointment. I was glad to see the friendly faces of the salon staff and I laughed and joked. I sat down, preparing myself for a half hour manicure. I was sitting very still, occasionally talking with my favorite manicurist while waiting for my favorite hairdresser. Ten minutes into the manicure two young and friendly looking police officers approached. They asked me to come with them. I saw Allen in the background. Boy, I figured, he must really be mad at me if he called the police this morning. Later I found out he had been extremely worried about me once he had cooled off.

His 911 call had been changed to a police alert for a "missing, disturbed person." This all broke down into a major mistake in terms of aggravation, money and time for Allen and me.

I thought the police would listen to my side of the events that transpired the previous evening, but I soon saw it was futile to try to convince them that things were now all right. They didn't take any notes as I spilled out my story in the police car as we headed downtown. We soon pulled into a vaguely familiar building. Why, for God's sake, this was the hospital where a month before my good gall bladder had been removed. If I was confined here, I would end my record of having stayed out of psychiatric wards for ten years! I would prefer a trip to headquarters and one phone call to this.

The police literally deposited me in the emergency room lockup. The wooden doors banged shut. The familiar panic set in. Were they going to needle me? A woman psychiatrist, dressed to the nines, came into the room and asked me a few questions. Then the lab performed a lithium level test. I later found out that my lithium level was better then normal. I was then left alone in the isolation room, not knowing what to expect next. Where was the massive dose of Thorazine? I got a real shock. No one came to ask questions or give me treatment for about five hours. There was no food, water or toilet facilities. I was forced to urinate on the floor. I couldn't comprehend what was happening. Had these people just forgotten about me? I managed to look through a crack in the room's one-door window. There were plenty of people coming and going outside. Many were laughing and talking. It appeared to me that they were having a high old time.

Finally, and not one moment too soon, the psychiatrist, a nurse and Allen arrived. Allen seemed so kind. I thought I was hallucinating. They were going to take me upstairs. Allen had my clothes. Okay. I'd go along with this. Maybe I'd get some food.

An entourage of guards, aides, and nurses accompanied us to the second floor psychiatric wing, a quiet place with obviously drugged patients painting ceramics. I sat down and started painting. That is basically all I remember of the next two days.

According to the hospital bill we later received, lots of Thorazine was needled into me. I do remember being strapped down to a bed—hands and legs. I must have been really fighting the Thorazine injections, trying to stay awake at all costs. All I know other than those nightmarish recollections is what Allen told me afterwards.

There was no comprehensive psychiatric facility in that hospital, just this little corner of the second floor. They had to transfer me (thank God) to the state hospital for treatment of my mania and for that I had to be committed by Allen. He, by this time, saw what they were doing to me—indiscriminate pills and shots—and conferred with my father. A state hospital in Decatur, Alabama, would take me if there was legal commitment. Allen signed the necessary papers. He saved my life.

Chapter 33

A LITTLE HOSPITAL
IN DECATUR or WE'RE JUST RNP
(REAL NICE PEOPLE)

"They" must have transferred me to the North Alabama Regional Hospital while I was drugged and asleep. I don't remember much about the first few days there except my fight with one of the mental health workers. I must have been breaking a rule, for he dragged me to my room. I resisted, of course. In the scuffle I apparently lost my upper temporary partial bridgework. It was never found, although I jokingly offer to pay ransom for it to the mental health worker who dragged me.

Nobody was hurt in the fight. At least I don't think the 250-pound man who moved me was seriously bruised. I later learned what an absolutely sweet guy that huge man was, like a big teddy bear. His heart just wasn't into manhandling anyone.

The general staff workers in this hospital were almost too nice for their own good. Boy, was I lucky to land there. Didn't I tell you Someone was looking out for me?

This hospital was extraordinary in many ways. The staff was fair. You got a fair deal. Democracy was practiced to a point. You could decide to refuse your medication if you didn't think it was suitable. I did that several times because of my nausea. Many other patients followed my example and turned down medications. I thought we were going to have a real problem, but somehow things got back on track. You received medicine by forced injection if you were unruly or out of control. You didn't get released from the hospital by refusing medication. That was the catch. Lockup consisted of only a single room and in the four weeks I was in this hospital, I never saw it used.

There was a music room, but its only music source, a radio, was broken. We did get a guitar and we had great pluckin' and singin'. Diana, a nurse with the voice of an angel, led the choir.

We also had classes. They ranged from instruction on our illnesses to my favorite, which was bell ringing. I became quite accomplished in ringing my bells in my portion of "Amazing Grace."

The patients were as wonderful as the staff. My roommate was Ma Jones, a real hillbilly with a gruff tone but a heart of gold. She frequently threatened to "whoop" me if I didn't behave. And she made good her promise. Being very fundamentalist, she believed the devil had something to do with it. She prayed to the Lord to make her better and He answered her.

While Ma Jones was my closest companion in the hospital, I spent much time with Charlotte (Charley), Joyce, and Will. Charley was 19 years old and was displaying physical manifestations of mania. She was on the move all the time. Noisy, happy, sweet, misunderstood. Joyce was depressed. Very depressed. I spent much time trying to build up her confidence but with little success. Will was a totally sweet manic who believed strongly in God's power and glory and felt he was supposed to spread the word. It felt odd being a listener for words I too had so often preached.

Most of the patients had been signed in by so-called loved ones, who promptly forgot about them. Allen didn't forget me. He phoned twice a day and brought dinner each evening and on weekends from nearby restaurants.

One of my fellow patients, Arthur, called me Peg Bundy after the television show character. He begged me to ask Al Bundy (Allen) to bring him a steak dinner. I told him that Al had his limits. Allen was very popular with almost all of my co-patients as he treated everyone with kindness and respect.

At first, I figured that this hospital was like all the rest and I acted accordingly. Sarcasm, flippant remarks, and negative behavior were my standard tactics. Since I was almost a professional at this game, I believe I did some damage to staff morale. They knew I was different—better educated than my fellow patients, used more sophisticated words than even most of the staff members, and had some money. Many of the mental health workers were usually broke, a poor reflection on where our society places its values.

I begged for two Alka Seltzers during my first week and a half in this hospital, since I continued to be extremely sick with stomach spasms and nausea. I even vomited on the floor of my room, thereby giving some credibility to my complaints of nausea. So I had two things to campaign for—new teeth and Alka Seltzer.

I put on quite a show, but even I had to admit it wasn't worth it. I was getting no closer to an appointment with the chief psychiatrist and possible release.

Enter the meek, repentant Judy. Sweet, reserved, non-theatrical; a real joy after all my trouble-making. The staff kept complimenting me on my rapid progress in recovering from my manic behavior. I let them think what they wanted. It was all one Judy. I already told you that I was an actress, and a good one, too.

Because of my new behavior, I was getting Alka Seltzer on request, and within a week I had a dental appointment to restore my lost partial, then a pass for the weekend followed by a two-week parole.

I will always remember Frank, Don, and all the others

who worked with me.

I don't know what the purpose of that hospital stay was. Maybe to heal my stomach (although no medicine was given for this purpose). Maybe to toughen me up for the years ahead. All I can say is that that hospital, where grade cards 1, 2, 3, and 4 meant advancement in patient privileges, and where the food was high fiber if not high in taste, was remarkable, simply remarkable. Thank you, God, for sending me there.

Chapter 34

I WALKED THROUGH THE VALLEY OF THE SHADOW OF DEATH AND KEPT ON WALKING

(Spring, 1996)

In 1996, Allen phoned the airlines to price shipping my remains to Philadelphia for burial. Most events of the time were blurred to me, selectively forgotten. Some I remembered, or learned about by reading a prematurely prepared epilogue written to close my story, and a letter of Allen's. He wrote that as therapy at the suggestion of my case worker. He was alarmingly depressed by the overwhelming negative happenings in our lives. Reading that letter shocked me to my senses.

Three hospitalizations in Huntsville left me confused. Then the serious one during our early months in Mobile (I told you about that in Chapter 1, when I lay down on a four-lane expressway) had almost ended my life. After that episode I had a few months reprieve. Then, despite my exaggerated optimism, I again became severely manic in March of 1996. That attack came even closer to ending my life. Despite my frequent badgering, Allen wouldn't describe events of that episode until several months after my recovery, when he believed I could take hearing them. I had voluntarily signed myself into the Mobile hospital because I'd been having all kinds of strange ideas. Foremost among them was that TV crews were waiting at the hospital to film the announcement of my running for election as the President of the United States. This was a time when I was trying hard to relearn Spanish to help me capture the Latino vote. I though this would excite TV viewers. I also thought that the film of this announcement session was going to be incorporated into a film biography of my life.

I was then and still am an idealist and dreamer. Only now can I see how warped my thoughts were then. In the throes of mania I stubbornly and impulsively formed dangerous, grandiose plans that wouldn't be surrendered or couldn't be dissipated without mental hospital confinement and treatment.

At the time, I was taking the prescribed dosage of Lithobid, my lithium medication, and biweekly tests showed I maintained an effective level in my blood. Yet, to achieve my goals, I was constantly running and wearing myself out and all those with whom I was in close contact. It was my manic-classical, hyper pattern of overacting. I was in the hospital lobby screaming for the TV crews when seven nurses, aides and security people moved in to transfer struggling me to the psychiatric ward. As soon as I was placed in restraints some staff members administered massive doses of lithium and sedatives.

Shortly after that, I later learned, I went into a deep coma. No one, at the time, knew what caused it, but all who were involved were alarmed. Certainly Allen was. After two days of tests and examinations, the battery of specialists concluded that my liver and pancreas had been destroyed by years of lithium accumulation. The massive lithium dose I had been given when brought into the psychiatric ward broke the camel's back, so to speak, and with the damaged liver and pancreas, a severe diabetic condition set in. Blood tests showed that I was suffering from both common types of diabetes. The coma lasted for six weeks, most of which had me hovering between life and death. I was being kept alive by an array of intravenous tubes giving me necessary fluids, medications and nourishment. Then, as if things weren't bad enough, one of the IV needles was contaminated and infected me. My temperature soared to 105 degrees and I was rushed from the psychiatric department to the hospital's critical care facility. Allen visited me there every day for nine days. On the tenth, day when he came into the room, I wasn't there. Thinking the worst had happened, and my body had been taken to the morgue, I'm told he nearly fainted. Fortunately, a nurse caught him and said, "If you're looking for Judy, she's been taken back to psychiatric." He found me still in a coma, but at least recovered from the severe infection.

There remain many unanswered questions about the coma. Many of the professionals attending me, with the exception of Dr. Ladd, believed that, because it had lasted so long, it would prove terminal. Some of them expressed this to Allen and suggested he begin investigating funeral arrangements. Dr. Ladd, however, convinced Allen that Electro Convulsive Therapy (ECT) held a promise for bringing me around. The interesting aspect of the proposal is that ECT was used as a treatment for mental conditions. How could that affect a diabetic liver and pancreas? Dr. Ladd's conclusion was that I had experienced two severe manic attacks in little more than three months, despite blood tests that showed I'd maintained a satisfactory lithium level. His conclusion was that my liver and pancreas had been accumulating the lithium for some time instead of releasing it to the brain where it would have kept me stable. As I could no longer be treated with lithium, and its replacements—Depakote and Tegritol—could only be administered orally, an impossibility while I was comatose, only two possibilities remained for my recovery. These were ECT or a likely fruitless watching and waiting.

Again, I was told that in spite of my abhorrence of the shock therapy I received in Austin, Allen consented to my receiving the ECT. Actually, it required 15 treatments in the last two weeks of the coma to return me to normal. A week after bolting upright and asking for my hairdresser I walked out of the hospital on my own two feet.

What had really happened? I firmly believe that the coma was God's way to correct all of my mistaken delusions and ideas. These had me taking things into my own hands in order to succeed in my stubbornly fanatical plans for achieving illogical goals. God wanted me to stop! The coma was His way of stopping me. During the six weeks of the coma, God talked to me firmly, but patiently.

There was to be no more arguing with Allen or anyone else for that matter. I was to "lay down my sword" and let Him fight for any aspirations I was meant to fulfill. Patience was to be my watchword. I questioned and argued with Him over these instructions, but in the end I capitulated. When I did so, the 15th ECT became the effective one for returning me from the shadow of the valley of death. I had walked through that valley, but had not stopped in it, for God had walked with me and talked with me. He had performed one of His many miracles, and I was in awe. He would not let Dr. Ladd give up on me. Dr. Ladd persisted in giving me one ECT after another. When I sat in Dr. Ladd's office weeks later and thanked him for his untiring efforts, he looked upward and said, "I had help."

The mysterious part about the whole episode is that, after I revived, doctors have found nothing wrong with my pancreas or liver, and all the glucose tolerance tests for diabetes Allen has been giving me for the past two years have shown normal levels.

So what really went on in that hospital? I don't know. Do you?

And Allen? About four months after I came out of the coma, I discovered the draft of a letter he had written while I was in the shadow world of a coma. Here it is in its entirety:

"Dear Friend: April 2, 1996

"I am confused. So if you are looking for determinitive answers there aren't any and this letter is not for you. It was written, however, to tell you that you are not alone if you have a closely related manic depressive and are torn on reaching decisions that will govern your and your loved one's futures.

"My wife is a manic depressive. She has been manic frequently and hospitalized 27 times. She was depressed only once, two months ago, in her 23 years of manifesting the disease. Judy became my wife almost 16 years ago following a whirlwind courtship stemming from 'love at first sight.' I have never lost that love. If I had I would likely not be so confused. Judy loses her love for me, I believe, when she is manic. Perhaps I am paranoid, but she couldn't treat me as hatefully and sadistically as she does when she is manic and still love me. Can her love for me return when she has recovered from a manic episode—a basic input for my confusion, my insecurity? Also adding to my confusion is my Puritan morality which keeps telling me, 'You knew Judy was manic when you were courting, willingly made a vow that you would stand by her in *sickness* and in health.' For 16 years, and through at least 10 of Judy's manic episodes, I kept that vow. Dealing with her eighth or ninth episode, successive episodes each having become more severe, my turmoil became so great that I developed high blood pressure. This condition became another input to my confusion, not a concern for myself but for how this, added to my other ailments, could lead to an early demise that would negatively affect Judy.

"Reading a recently published autobiography, *An Unquiet Mind*, by Kay Redfield Jamison, alleviated a little of my confusion. I recommend it to you. Kay Jamison's story impressed upon me that Judy's manic and depressive characteristics, symptoms and behavior—even when she is functioning supposedly normally—are characteristic; that there are hundreds of thousands of persons in these United States who are just like her; that your manic depressive and mine are not unique but are just two more of these numbers. (Is there comfort in numbers?) Pertinent to this, I also learned, with some relief, that I had been intuitively handling Judy as properly as could be expected from a layman; that the operative action on my part has been in giving her love by deed, word and expression since we first met. Giving love is easy to do when you sincerely feel it. When you don't, and it is definitely difficult to show love for a manic person who is abrasive and abusive to you, faking it becomes an effective action. After all, the will to deliberately pursue faking under adverse circumstances can be another form of love.

"*An Unquiet Mind* also gave me a very disquieting input. A manic depressive's episodes of disturbance can become more frequent and intense with time. I had previously heard this from one or two mental health professionals but didn't appreciate its significance *for me*, so ignored it. I didn't want to believe it because I thought 'Judy is different.' After all, hadn't she once gone nearly ten years without an attack? Her present manic episode, which is alarmingly severe, is her third in the past half year—quite an input! All of these type situations are recounted in *An Unquiet Mind*; the increase in attack frequency, the increase in attack severity, and remissions of long duration.

"Something doesn't apply from Kay Jamison's story, however. It's an unusual and unfortunate distinction that has Judy standing out from the thousands of other manic depressives. After many years of successful response to lithium treatments, Judy is no longer achieving good benefit from that medication. Her present attack took place despite her having a (slightly) elevated blood lithium level, not as in the past, when she stopped taking her lithium so that she could feel euphoric, genius-endowed and God-designated. Lithium is a wonder drug. Despite some of its side effects it's as essential for manic depressives as is water. But what is to be done if lithium no longer works, if a 'lithium tolerance' has been developed? What can be done with Judy? Too much confusion, too few inputs.

"Before I continue regarding my confusion and inputs to my confusion—am I being obsessive with these two words?—I need to provide some background. Manic depression is an old disease, likely as old as humankind. But it has been studied and recognized significantly only in our present half century. Some victims of the disease like to recount the famous people who had and have it—Winston Churchill, Thomas Edison, Vivien Leigh, Patty Duke, Ernest Hemingway, Mozart, Donald Trump. We seldom hear of the thousands of everyday victims, of course. Manic depression has been receiving close medical attention, in actuality, for only the past 10-15 years. One recent step, and I'll let you judge its worth, was to overcome the stigma associated with the word manic by now terming the disease 'bipolar disorder.' Far more significant has been the development of lithium substitutes and supplements, including Tegratol and Depakote, and the focused development of shock treatments. The term 'shock treatments' also bears a stigma from movies of the '30s and '40s, horror stories and tales of police state tortures. With its development focused for the treatment of bipolar disorders and schizophrenia, it became Electroconvulsive Therapy, or ECT. Both the old and new terms convey equally unpleasant images as far as I am concerned, but if it works, what's in a name?

"It is now reported that Judy is not responding well to the new medications and ECT is being considered. If ECT is unsuccessful, it is possible that Judy will have to be permanently institutionalized. These are obviously serious inputs for my consideration and even the basis for my confusion.

"I keep using the word 'input' for fact or factor because I have been trained in science and practiced it for nearly 50 years. Scientists neatly collect and collate their inputs (facts or factors that are given values) and weigh them in solving problems. These inputs concerning Judy do not permit a neatly solved package, however, and this leads to my confusion. Love and other emotions; the primevally inherent concerns for self-preservation and esteem; a person's aspirations, abilities, capabilities and spiritual beliefs cannot be assigned succinct weighted values. Therefore, my friend, if you can quantify such human factors for clarifying your thinking regarding your bipolar loved one, do so before you are overwhelmed. You should already have all of the important facts at hand should you take the time to seriously think about it. Quantify the new incoming factors only to discard them as being insignificant, or to adjust the mechanics for behaviors and actions you have already *objectively appreciated* as called for on your behalf. I am far from wealthy but I do recognize that financial factors need be suppressed in any deliberations. Financial problems can only increase when a loved one is permitted to continue on a destructive course.

"If what I have just written has positive application to your problem you are fortunate. I do not believe my situation can be readily solved with a minimum of hurt to both Judy and me. It's inputs are:

"Despite her behavior during her manic episodes, I know that Judy and I deeply love one another. When she is not having an attack, our mutual companionship is of a storybook nature. We are a team that thrives on togetherness. But I am almost 20 years older than Judy and am suffering several serious ailments. It is likely that I will predecease her. That I truly love Judy suggests that I should now let her go her own way so that she can learn to function independent of me while she is young enough to do so. With her disease (and bipolar disorder is an incurable disease), it is logical that Judy should relocate to the one area where she has friends and family to take care of her during her *inevitable* future attacks. This location is almost 1500 miles away. For health reasons I need to stay near or where we now reside. My condition does not permit lengthy auto or air travel. Because we would have a great distance between us and

Judy should be free to seek a life without me, is our divorcing in order? Am I rationalizing this because I'm afraid that my health no longer permits me to contend with Judy's manic episodes?

"We have no family or friends where we now reside. If we were not to divorce and remain in this location there is a pessimistic possibility that another attack of Judy's could see her permanently committed to a local institution. I certainly wouldn't be able to care for her or visit with her if her manic attack was to lead to my having a stroke or heart attack, both being possibilities. Looking further to the future, when I am gone, who would there then be to care for and visit with Judy in an institution? We have no friends or family who would. Sould Judy be permanently institutionalized it would be best that this be somewhere near able friends and family members. Now may be the best time to prepare for such an eventuality.

"Being objective, my reasons for not separating from Judy are selfish. I crave her presence, her affection. I feel fulfilled when I am taking care of her. I remember my marriage vow. That may seem inconsequential to you, but it is important to me. I need Judy to take care of me, partic ularly with my deteriorating condition. The devil on my shoulder says, 'You took care of her through many manic attacks and other illnesses. Now it's her turn to take care of you.' But Judy can't take care of me if she is confined for her disorder or even if she's building up to a severe episode. Such a build-up could extend over months. After reading the above, do you want to exchange problems?

"Well, friend, from my letter you can appreciate that a close relationship with a person having bipolar disorder entails many complex problems. Try to gain comfort from the fact that you are not alone. Neither your situation nor your loved one's is unique. But because humans vary tremendously your problems and inputs for decision-making could have aspects that also vary tremendously from those of others. However, there will be 'common denominators' coming out of the professionals' new research in the understanding and treatment of bipolar disorder. Communicate with the professionals who are helping your loved one. They know that your actions and clear thinking, leading to your well-being, are also essential elements in effecting the cure of your loved one. Their primary interest is to realize this cure, even though it may be temporary. As professionals, however, their secondary interest is in helping you, for your benefit as well as that of your loved one. You are not alone.

"With empathy,

"Allen M. Feder"

* * *

I read this letter four months after recovering from the coma. It scared me at first. What a horrible prognosis! I hated all its negativeness and the fact that it inferred that I was some stereotype. I read it over and over again trying to learn how to avoid the picture Allen painted. I actually resolved that the manic pictured by Allen would not be me. And I have succeeded, I believe, in turning my life into a very positive and productive one.

Chapter 35

ECTs

Dr. Ladd was very concerned that I would soon suffer another manic episode. Lithium as a preventative had proved disastrous. Dr. Ladd said, "We'll now try Tegretol and Depakote and hope for good results." At our next meeting, after persevering for two weeks with each of these medications, I was extremely sick with nausea and gagging. Dr. Ladd shook his head with worry. Then he smiled, "We'll keep this mania under control with ECTs."

Allen and I looked at each other. What did that mean for me? I soon found out. For five months, at three week intervals, I was given out-patient ECTs. The objective was to prevent recurrences of severe mania and hospitalizations. At this point I was ready to try anything to avoid hospitalizations and the inevitable lockups.

Dr. Ladd would brief me the day before I was to have an ECT. "You can take your sleeping medication before 11:00 p.m., but no food or drink after midnight. Under the anesthetic any food or fluids in your stomach could be regurgitated into the lungs with fatal results. If you get too thirsty, try sucking ice cubes. See you tomorrow morning, Mrs. Feder."

These instructions were difficult to adhere to. I'd go to sleep early the night before the therapy but invariably awaken at midnight. Without having a beverage, I found it impossible to return to sleep.

3:00 a.m.: The apartment is totally in darkness. I could watch no television, listen to no radio, or scribble no notes. I had to be as quiet as a mouse. Allen, remembering past preludes to my manic attacks, could be upset if he awoke and found me doing any of these things in the middle of the night. But the boredom and tiredness were sometimes overwhelming.

5:30 a.m.: Allen's alarm clock sounded. At least now I'd be able to turn on a light. How Allen managed to follow the early morning routine that interfered with his medications schedule I'll never know. He and I, being in our own dazes, talked very little. We just concentrated on getting me to the hospital for the ECT routine.

7:15 a.m.: I was wheel-chaired down a long, bland corridor to the treatment room. Here I was greeted by a nurse handing a denture cup to me. "Put your false teeth in here," she said with stark professionalism. "And here's a hospital gown for you." Miserably, I would undress and put on the hospital gown. The bad memories I have of previous experiences in which I had to dress in a hospital gown made me feel worse.

7:30 a.m.: I lay on a gurney waiting until the other patients were treated. The 7:30 a.m. schedule always had me the last victim for the day's ECTs, which was Dr. Ladd's consideration for Allen's medication schedule. Now it was my turn.

7:45 a.m.:The anesthesiologist's nurse inserted an IV into my arm. Shortly after, Dr. Ladd walked in, came to my gurney, and took my hand. "Hey, Mrs. Feder," he said. By this time the anesthetic was taking effect. "Hey, Dr. Ladd," I mumbled. My eyes closed and the preventative ECT was administered.

8:30 a.m.: "Where am I," I asked? "You're in the hospital," a nurse replied. "You just had your treatment and your husband is waiting for you. Let's get dressed." I had a monstrous headache, couldn't remember anything and could barely dress and stand.

A nurse's aide wheeled me to Allen, who was waiting in the hospital lobby. Reliable Allen. I felt as bad as I could ever remember feeling. The ECT had definitely slowed me down and destroyed my short term memory in the process. I was achingly tired, irritable, and my speech was slurred.

9:30 a.m.: Home again. My bed felt soft, smooth and comforting. "Allen, Honey, I'll just take a little nap. I'm going to make it. Please don't leave me alone now."

For five months, that was the scenario; horrible! I became aware of the consequences of "inappropriate behavior." It didn't take much for me to realize that the ECT routine was unacceptable and intolerable for me. I made up what was left of my mind to end the need for outpatient ECTs, manic-suppressing medications and their alternatives, mental ward confinements. I started looking for ways to stop the cycle.

By chance (?) I met a wonderful person, Lana Kershner. She was a nurse, but now is engaged in education. When we met she was enthusiastically preparing a course on common sense, morals and ethics for Alabama public school students (and their teachers). She was loaded down with posters, cartoons and other illustrations of homey, everyday advice. A brief first inspection of her messages convinced me that they could help me change my behavior, become a new person, or at least a better one. I jumped on Lana's bandwagon. I sat for long hours leafing through the many folders of her sayings, all the time thinking of how I could apply them. I knew that adhering to certain of these would change what had been the downhill course of me life. At the same time I began a new strategy with Allen. He would have no more of my nagging, yelling and complaining. He would no longer be able to accuse me of being manic or just irritable. He would no longer have need to confer with Dr. Ladd as to my need for another ECT. The new strategy made for a happy Allen, and a happy Allen made a happier me.

Dr. Ladd was amazed that my study and adherence to certain of Lana's aphorisms, as he called these words of advice, were slowing me down—I was thinking before I spoke and looking before I leaped. Lana's teaching materials emphasized health, patience, attitude, creativity and self control (e.g. If you don't control yourself, someone else will). I could understand Lana's teachings and liked what I was getting from them, success in improving my life. One month without an ECT. Next, six months since the last one. Then 18 months! Dr. Ladd described my change in behavior as being "remarkable and amazing." For months now in our sessions he has not mentioned medications or preventive ECTs. He has credited much of the change in me to my willpower. I was proud when I heard this, for willpower is a quality I didn't even guess I possessed.

The path I had followed for 26 years was very winding. There were many forks and obstacles in the road. Finally, Dr. Ladd said, "It's all smooth sailing for you now. You can appreciate the simplicity and ease of things that will from now on happen to you." I appreciated this and have acquired a special motto, "Moderation in all things." I know that if I don't want another of those incredibly horrible ECTs I must keep my act together. For this I sometimes have to be an actress to play a new role in my life, a role for making a new Judy. I must be doing a good acting job because Dad, Allen, Dr. Ladd, and Jamie are all happy with me and trusting me. That trusting is the very best thing of all.

Sometimes someone asks, "How did you overcome all of the obstacles and recover?" My response is, "I recollected and studied my past failures and achievements. From this I learned to eliminate all that was bad and salvaged all that was good." Old habits were hard to break, but I did so. In turn, I could now recognize and form new and better ones. The success of growing into the new me makes me feel good. Thank you God for all you have given me.

Chapter 36

ON BEING PRODUCTIVE

I've told you about the terrors of my manic episodes. But luckily for me they were always followed by a return to normalcy. During the years between attacks I struggled to find something meaningful and constructive to do to occupy the long hours. This was difficult because my prescribed medication made me extremely tired. I just had to find activities that would occupy what was left of my brain.

I deeply missed teaching, particularly interacting with my students. But I was forced to face the fact that, with my decreased energy levels, effective teaching was an impossibilty.

To make up for the resulting void, I began to write. Not the scribbled chicken tracks that I'd written when manic, but attempts to logically relate my ideas on paper concerning education, health, politics, etc.

I started with my educational strategies and methods. Allen typed up all my notes into what he titled, "An Holistic Approach to Improving Education." Many classroom memories returned, and I was finding fulfillment with this project. So, with no marketing plan in mind, I mailed copies to the superintendents of major school systems. Both Alabama and Texas superintendents responded favorably. But the problem remained of how to implement my ideas. It still remains, and only time will tell what becomes of all this effort.

My "non-manic" dream is to help upgrade education and make learning more fun by discovery approaches. Maybe, just maybe, I'll get a chance to influence teaching methods. But sending my writings to Hillary Clinton is just plain futile. The non-manic Judy realizes that things take time, and all we can do is plant the seed. Where and when it will grow is beyond our control.

I've had several "Letters to the Editor" published on topics ranging from our national debt, to the ancient Greeks, to God's role in influencing the weather.

Perhaps my greatest accomplishment is slowing down enough to write this autobiography. My cousin Frank read the rough draft and kept congratulating me on the "clarity." "But," he admonished, "it'll never sell."

"Why?" I asked.

"Because there's no sex or violence."

Well, at least I wanted to be President. What a crazy idea! Who would want the job anyway?

Chapter 37

HEALTHIER AND WISER

After my miraculous cure and having been saved from death, I decided that it was about time to pay more attention to my health. It felt so good to be alive and out of hospitals that I made up my mind to try my best to keep it that way. I had been trying for years to lead a healthier life. Now I would make a serious attempt to put into practice certain ideas and philosophies I'd developed.

My dream to be thin led me to deplorable eating habits which definitely affected my nerves. Now was the time to change. I planned new menus for a new life. I substituted fruits for chocolate candy, grain cereals for cookies, and wheat bread for white bread.

I decided to use my common sense to see if I could achieve good health. I drank lots of fluids (iced tea is my one addiction), used vitamin supplements, stuck to the high fiber foods I'd been touting ever since I lost a dear, young and talented friend to colon cancer, and pursued a scheduled exercise plan. This regime, plus a positive outlook toward the goal of being "the best I could be," proved successful. (The only glitch in my plan is that drinking copious amounts of fluids violates one of my favorite aphorisms, "Everything in moderation."). I no longer alternately starve myself, then binge. My meals include lots of fruits, vegetables, and grains. I'm not hungry all the time because these can be filling without being high in calories. Diet shots and pills are things of the past for me.

I am not a size eight and probably never will be. My body frame has given me a size 12 figure that I appreciate because my health is excellent. This makes me happy and content so that I want to share this success with others. The "secret" is to start slowly, experiment carefully with the mentioned food types, and above all, heed the aphorism, "Everything in moderation." God gave each of us a unique and miraculous body that is a great blessing. It is essential to take proper care of it. I learned the hard way, that a "Sound mind needs a sound body." If I may quote a sermon I once heard:

"We can not pray to God to end disease. He has already given us minds and skills to search our cures and healing, if only we use them constructively."

During another of my bouts with the devil, mania, I decided to open a comprensive health studio and franchise it globally. I had found another way to save mankind.

I don't remember what the graphic that follows was for—advertising, client instruction or what. I have saved it both to remind me of some of the grandiouse delusions I have had when experiencing mania, and, to tell the truth, even when normal I believe the comprehensive health studio concept has potential.

Moderation in All Things
Nothing to Excess

THE TOTAL YOU,
THE HEALTHY YOU

A Sound Mind in a Sound Body

Eat to Live, Not Live to Eat
Be The Best You Can Be!

COMPILED BY:
JUDY K. FEDER

Chapter 38

CHRISTMAS 1997

I received a Christmas card from a good friend in 1997. He wrote, "May 1998 be the year of the Feders." A very nice thought, indeed. Actually, 1997 was a pretty good year for us. I'm healing. The wounds are closing. My mind is recovering and my memory is coming back.

Finally, I'm beginning to develop a plan for my life. I'm going to take one day at a time and make each day count and be a happy one. (The greatest blessing that will bring is that it will make Allen happy, too.) I'm learning to constantly maintain control of myself. Brutal experience has proved that when I lose control, unpleasant things happen. Let me summarize for you the essence of my new self-control:

While none of us can guarantee our future, during the past two years I have developed a knowledge and control of my bipolar condition that has provided me complete confidence that I will never again be a mental hospital patient. The roots of this confidence, the gaining of knowledge permitting it, are related to the close of my story. The control I mentioned is simple. First and foremost, using prescribed medication, I insure my getting a minimum of eight hours of sleep nightly. Second, at any time during the day, should I experience the least feelings of over-excitement or frustration, I take half (2.5 mg) of the mildest Valium tablet (5.0 mg) available. If within half an hour of this I am not satisfied that I have returned to reasonable calmness, I take the other half of the tablet. This, and Allen's comforting attention has proved effective for the past two years. But I possess still another very important element of control that, at this writing, I have yet to employ. That is the knowledge that if the prelude to mania continues, I can receive, with just a few hours notice, an outpatient ECT. Although this would briefly block my short term memory, it would return me to full control well within 24 hours.

I must learn to think things out before I act, and to spot the very earliest signs of mania. By now the recognizable signs, such as a buying spree, irritability, lack of sleep, loss of appetite, compulsive grandios planning, exceedingly excess energy, can be combated early and kept within good limits. The basic idea is to pursue moderation in all aspects of my life and to let Allen help me all he can. He can see patterns of behavior that aren't always apparent to me. By 1998, my regular visits with Dr. Ladd had become a joy. I'd been off ECT's for months and the good doctor didn't even mention "preventative" ECT any more. He, too, believed moderation was the key word.

The other important part of staying well is exhibiting great patience. When I was sick I wanted to fulfill all my (delusional) schemes immediately. I raced from one plan to the next without analyzing, questioning or thinking about the possible results of my actions. This led to disaster. Wisdom comes from learning from our mistakes and achievements. God has given each of us the tools we need to reach our potential, but it is up to each of us to figure out the best way to utilize them. Everyone needs a plan and some goals.

I wake up every day now with a feeling of eagerness. What does God have in store for me? How soon will His tapestry unravel? Dr. Ladd said that I had "made it to the mountaintop, yet I was still grounded with one foot on the earth." He also said that there are a few forks in the road up there, adding, "You're showing clarity and insight into your past and present." He concluded, "You're remarkable, Mrs. Feder. You've turned all my ideas about mania upside down. Keep up the good work."

I don't feel remarkable. Every day is a challenge to remain stable and calm. I've always seen things as I want them to be, not as they are. Finally, I am dealing with reality but also with an optimistic note for the future. I am now convinced that every problem has a cure—often several possible solutions. It is up to me to weigh, evaluate and choose each appropriate course of action. As a history teacher, I view Judy Feder's history as a prologue to the present and future. Curiosity, amazement, skepticism, and hope all fill my head. Are two people alike? Do I fall into a category, or can I achieve a healthy, unique personality? Slowly but surely I will use my common sense and work and wait for the answers.

I am grateful for my new circumstances. I have been told by Dr. Ladd, family and friends that I am again expressing creativity and being innovative as I was 25 years ago. Allen says I am a unique combination of historian, educator, and problem solver. The lithium and Thorazine I was dosed with for so many years had dulled my ability to think my way through a doorway. The ECTs would wipe out my short term memory to an extent that Allen would have to help me find the bedroom when he brought me home from a treatment. In summary, I feel again ready to strive for achieving my potential as soon as God has set it for me. We *do,* and then we hear.

I need to logically and properly channel my energy to accomplish what has yet to be destined for me. My learning period occupied my last 26 years of mistakes and achievements.

For now, I am glad to be free from sickness and delusions. My main goal is to repay all Allen's love and loyalty and above all determine who is Judy Feder, and what are her strong points and credentials.

I am still trying to discover the right path that I have to take. But I am still young and there is no longer any time pressure. "Haste makes waste."

If I cannot find the way, I will then trust Him to help me make one.

Chapter 39

A FAMILY REUNION

January, 1998

My daughter and her beautiful, white Laborador retriever, Shelby, visited us early in the year, three months after Allen fell and tore his right shoulder muscle. The second day of Jamie's visit, Allen again fell, that time breaking his left arm in two places. With both his arms in slings he was totally dependent on me. If you recall, that was one of the concerns he expressed in the letter he wrote when I was in a coma. It was a fear that proved groundless. Even through Allen's discomfort, I maintained continuing self-control, handled the stress of the additional workload his injuries placed on me.

Despite Allen's mishap, we all managed to rescue Jamie's and Shelby's visit, and made it memorable for pleasant reasons. A few days after our guests departed I received a letter:

"Dear Mom:
"Each day I was with you, you seemed to get stronger than the day before. It's good to see you doing so well. I still worry, but that's only because I've done it for so long that it's hard to stop, but I'll work on it. As far as

the memories from the past go, I'm glad you've forgotten most of them. It's better that way and I'll try to do the same."

Happy Days are Here Again!

Two broken arms won't ruin our reunion. Allen and Jamie.

Doggonit, it's fun being together. Judy and her daughter Jamie with Shelby.

Chapter 40

I'M FREE AGAIN, I'M ME AGAIN!

It is difficult to end my story when I feel that my life is just beginning. My 52nd birthday was April 19, 1998. Fifty-two is relatively young. I now feel no pressure to achieve my goals. My new motto is, "Patience is not indifference; Watch, work and wait." Heeding this is giving me a beautiful, relaxed life, something I rarely enjoyed since that first manic attack. I still occasionally slip into impatience and irritability, but Allen is always there for me. Allen, Dad, Dr. Ladd and my aphorisms are the tools for my staying mentally and physically healthy. The change in my mental condition came about with my learning when and how to use these tools. They are now the essential parts of my new life and I must never forget to use them properly.

Having to fight mania requires that I now pursue a totally new approach to life. I've discovered means for combating the illness that works for me, and perhaps will for others. But I have to be constantly on guard to employ these means as needed. Treating the earliest appearance of the symptoms, and not letting them progress is much better than having an attack. With receiving the proper amounts of love and my positive thinking, moderation and control I believe that I can win my never ending struggle. Also, I will take 0.25 mg Valium when I'm beginning to feel irritable which now, thank God, doesn't happen very often. (Taking an occasional, mild dose of Valium is a lot better than being in a mental ward and daily getting shot with 1,000 mg of Thorazine.) In all, my new approach is working for me!

Life without hospitalizations and ECTs is great. Every day I appreciate this more. I'm free! I'm free to drive my car, free to go walking, free to use my cosmetics and hair dryer— none of these having been permitted during my hospitalizations. Most important is that the new me is free to use my ability to help other people. That's what this book is all about.

Allen and I have developed into a team. We work together, for example, as public radio volunteer broadcasters reading local newspapers for the visually impaired. I also give presentations to mental health organizations and participate in the activities of two writers' groups. My booklet of aphorisms is nearing publication. It is geared to help people facing adversity, as was I. (The aphorism I believe most pertinent for continuing as the new me is, "Control yourself, or others will.")

In all, things are really looking up and life is great! I appreciate that it's my attitudes that count the most. I know that there have been and will be (hopefully minor) setbacks. Also I know that life with health and freedom is great. Now that Allen trusts me and doesn't have to worry about me all of the time he has a new freedom too!

Thank you, God, Dr. Ladd, Allen and Dad for helping my recovery. I do know, however, that I'm in a never-ending battle, and even with all my allies, truly winning is up to me.

Dr. Gilbert R. Ladd IV and Judy Feder.

Delusional, For God's Sake!